Pheme
Perkins

PAUL in ASIA MINOR

The Life and Letters of Paul

Abingdon Press
Nashville

PAUL IN ASIA MINOR

Copyright © 2001 by Abingdon Press

This book is printed on acid-free paper.

ISBN 0-687-09093-8

01 02 03 04 05 06 07 08 09 10 — 10 9 8 7 6 5 4 3 2 1

Manufactured in the United States of America

CONTENTS

HOW TO USE
THIS RESOURCE

Welcome to *Paul in Asia Minor*, an eight-session study on Paul's letters of Philemon, Colossians, and Ephesians and his relationship with these congregations in Asia Minor. Each of the eight chapters contains common elements designed to help you use this resource successfully in a group setting or as a personal study.

"Read Colossians"

First you will note throughout each chapter that there are a number of subheadings that direct you to read a portion of Paul's letter. While there may also be cross references to numerous other passages in the Bible, the subhead passage is the key to the lesson. If this is an individual endeavor, you can read the Bible references as you encounter them.

Convenient Short Blocks of Text

Second you will find that the subheadings break up text into segments that are usually about two-to-three pages long. While the information in the chapter forms a coherent whole, the ideas are "sized" so that you can not only take the long view but also spend time with distinct ideas within the whole.

Study Questions

At the end of each of these divisions within the chapter are study and discussion questions and activities that relate to that segment of the text. Many of the questions are designed to make sure you understand the biblical text. Colossians and Ephesians can be complicated pieces of Scripture, and the apostle's argument may sound foreign or confusing to 21st-century culture.

Other questions are more analytical and ask readers to assess meanings for the original audience. That understanding leads to another level of study helps: personal reflection on what the revealed meaning of the biblical passage means and how those learnings and faithful insights can be applied to one's life.

Closing

At the end of each chapter are some suggestions for closing that apply to both a group and an individual setting. Many times you will be asked to summarize the content and import of that chapter and the selected Scripture. In each instance, you are invited to a time of prayer.

Leading a Group

If you are leading a group, these pointers will help you plan the study session:

• Read the entire chapter, including all the Scriptures. At least read the Scriptures related to the particular letter of Paul that is the subject of that chapter. Reading the cross references will be very helpful in getting a broader view.

- Think about your group members: their needs, their experience with the Bible and with each other, their questions. From this information, establish one or two session goals.

- Pay particular attention to the study questions and select at least one or two questions, if possible, from each segment of the text. Keeping in mind your group and your goals, note which questions you intend to cover. Try to have a variety of content, analytical, and personal application questions and activities.

- Encourage group members to use their Bibles and to read these texts.

- Be comfortable with silence and give group members a chance to think. Be sure that no one dominates and that everyone has the opportunity to participate.

- Have an intentional closure to the session by engaging in the suggested prayer or other spiritual discipline.

- Accept our best wishes and blessings for a transformational and edifying study time.

INTRODUCTION

The region of Asia Minor was home to the three letters of Philemon, Colossians, and Ephesians, which are the subject of this volume. Philemon was a prominent Christian living, probably, in Colossae; this letter is the only undisputed letter of Paul to an individual.

There is some doubt about the authenticity of Colossians and more so of Ephesians as distinctly Pauline letters. Pseudonymous writing was commonplace in that era; to write a letter in the name of a respected and prominent patron was considered neither dishonest nor uncomplimentary. To the contrary, it was an accepted practice.

Colossae and Ephesus were prominent cities in what is now modern Turkey. These letters will take you inside Paul's heart and his theology, as well as his life in and around Ephesus. Some of his time there was spent in prison. The extent of his liberty, or lack of liberty, can be pieced together from the clues throughout these letters and from corresponding information in the Book of Acts and other Pauline letters.

Cross References

This study includes numerous cross references to Acts and to Pauline correspondence other than these three letters, but it also takes into account several historical and extra-biblical sources. You will encounter references, for example, to Philo and Tacitus, writers of the first-century church era. You will also find several citations from the Apocrypha, books that are considered outside the accepted canon for most Protestant denominations, but included in the Holy Scriptures for the Roman Catholic and Eastern Orthodox churches, among others. In addition, at least one cross reference is drawn from the Pseudepigrapha, extra-biblical books written during the Intertestamental period. While these notations provide a broader background for the biblical text, they are not necessary to understanding the study material.

Family Matters

Perhaps one of the most prominent themes throughout these letters is the attention to family matters, both in the natural family and in the household of faith. Paul (or his anonymous disciple-writer) exhorts, encourages, nudges, cajoles, entreats, and warns members of Christian families and Christian communities on the benefits, dangers, responsibilities, and blessings of living a Spirit-filled life. They are at every turn reminded of Paul's stellar example of faith, particularly in the context of hardship, and how to live out their own authentically committed and devout life for the sake of Christ.

This example by Paul is not a time-bound image. Indeed, there is much to commend to the modern believer a life of intelligent discipline, faithful support, and mutual encouragement—all toward the goal of building up the body of Christ.

I CHRISTIAN FAMILY MATTERS

From Prison to House Church
Read Philemon 1-3

What can we learn from the opening of a letter? The rules for letterhead and address require the name of the sender(s), recipients, and a greeting. All Paul's letters change the standard Greek form, "greeting" (from a word related to "grace" and the Jewish "peace"), to "grace and peace." Paul also links the "Lord Jesus Christ" with God as the source of peace. So we know that Paul writes to fellow Christians when he uses this form of greeting (verse 3).

The names in the address tell us something, too. Study of ancient letters shows that the term _brother_ can be used between associates or friends. It does not always point to a family relationship. Similarly, the expression "dear friend" or "beloved" is a set form of address. It can be used even when the contents of a letter show that the sender and recipient are hostile to each other. But Paul has added some special notes to tell us a bit more about Philemon and Archippus. They have both played a part in spreading the gospel. The expressions "co-worker" and "fellow soldier" are equivalent terms for associates in Paul's mission of preaching and church building (see Philippians 2:25).

Timothy, Paul's co-sender (also 2 Corinthians 1:1;

Philippians 1:1; Colossians 1:1), often served as Paul's emissary to churches (see 1 Corinthians 4:17; 16:10; Philippians 2:19). The addressees must have gotten to know Timothy when they were converted by Paul's preaching. Since no designation except "our sister" is given Apphia, she is probably Philemon's wife (compare the couples in Romans 16:3, 7, 15). Colossians 4:17 reminds Archippus to complete a task that he has undertaken for the mission. Therefore, it seems likely that Philemon, Apphia, and Archippus reside in Colossae. Paul also addresses a church in "your" (singular), that is, Philemon's house. Some interpreters think that Archippus must be related to Philemon and Apphia, perhaps their son.

The missionary activity of Philemon and the others probably involved gathering a community of believers to establish that house church. Paul does not appear to have established the faith in Colossae himself (Colossians 1:6-7; 2:1) but may have passed through the city on journeys from Galatia or Phrygia to Ephesus (Acts 18:23; 19:1). Where Philemon met and was converted by Paul (Philemon 10), we do not know.

Although Paul expects this letter to be made known to the church in Philemon's house, it concerns a private matter, the relationship between Philemon and one of his house slaves, Onesimus. Contrary to his usual custom, Paul does not invoke his commission as "apostle" in the address (compare Romans 1:1; 1 Corinthians 1:1; Colossians 1:1). In the body of the letter, we see Paul asking, pleading, and attempting to persuade Philemon to receive Onesimus as a beloved fellow Christian. Paul refrains from commanding particular behavior.

Instead of any honorific or missionary title, Paul refers to himself simply as "prisoner of Christ Jesus" (Philemon 1).

That opens up another puzzle. Was the Letter to Philemon written from jail in Caesarea (Acts 2:33) or in Rome (Acts 28:16)? Both locations seem too great a distance from Colossae for Paul to be mediating between master and slave in Colossae or for Paul's expectation that he will soon be released and stay with Philemon (Philemon 22). As a result, many scholars think that Paul's references to imprisonments (2 Corinthians 11:23) and mortal peril in Asia (1 Corinthians 15:32; 2 Corinthians 1:8) indicate that he was imprisoned in Ephesus earlier in his ministry. During this period he received aid from the church at Philippi (Philippians 2:19-30; 4:10-20).

What did it mean to be a prisoner in the Greco-Roman world? Imprisonment was not a form of punishment. Persons being held were either waiting to have their cases disposed of, as in Paul's case here, or to have a sentence of death, exile, or forced labor carried out. Wealthy, prominent persons might be permitted a form of relaxed house arrest, as in Acts 28:16. Prisoners could also be held by guards in a fortress, as in Acts 23:33-35. Slaves and lower class criminals might be forced to endure more severe confinement and be chained and beaten (Acts 16:22-24).

The fact that Paul was allowed to have visitors and could correspond with several churches suggests that his imprisonment was not of the severest kind. However, one should not forget that guards often demanded bribes from family or friends who wished to visit prisoners. Study of the penal system leads scholars to question the usual view that Onesimus had been picked up as a runaway slave (*fugitivus*), met Paul in jail by chance, was converted, and was sent back to his master with Paul's letter to moderate Philemon's wrath. Instead, they believe that Onesimus would have had to make an effort—and probably paid bribes—to seek out Paul. Therefore, he must have known of Paul's influence with his master and perhaps had heard Paul in his master's company.

FROM PRISON TO HOUSE CHURCH

• "Read the address and content line before opening any electronic mail": our advice to avoid crashing the computer with a deliberate virus. "I never read that stuff," a colleague said. Do you read the address of letters, whether paper or e-mail?

• Read the opening of Paul's letters. Compare Philemon 1-3 and Philippians 1:1-2, 2 Corinthians 1:1-2, Colossians 1:1-2 where Timothy is also mentioned. Notice the differences in how Paul speaks of himself. What term does he use to sum up who he is in each case? What is Paul's relationship to the addressees?

• My "current occupant" mail or batch e-mail is trashed or deleted immediately. What about Paul's letters? Are they "mail" you wish to receive? Or are they closer to "junk mail"?

• Look at the "To . . ." part of Philemon (verses 1-2). How does Paul grab the reader's attention?

• Besides telling us that two men and a woman have worked with him, he adds, "to the church in your [Philemon's] house." Would that get you to go on reading? Or does it feel like a "current occupant" line?

Thanksgiving for a Christian
Read Philemon 4-7

The ordinary private letter expressed thanks for the health or well-being of the recipients. Paul develops this convention into a longer prayer report in which he expresses thanks for the Christian faith of the recipients (Philemon 4-7; see also Romans 1:8-15; 1 Corinthians 1:4-9; Philippians 1:3-11). The thanksgivings are not purely formal, since each points forward to the particular situation of Paul's addressees. (Paul's omission of any thanksgiving at the beginning of Galatians underlines the crisis facing that church.) So as we read the words of praise in Paul's thanksgiving for Philemon, we should anticipate that Paul will call on those same virtues in the body of the letter.

Ancient Mediterranean culture governed social behavior through appeal to honor and shame. This code was quite unlike our individualized "self-esteem," since honor depended upon what others said about you. Nor was honor merely personal. It attached to families, to all those connected to a particular household, and to cities. Individuals had to act in ways that enhanced the honor of the family, social group, and city state to which they belonged. Societies that still operate by this code often exact punishments for dishonorable behavior (which seems irrational to us) because shameful behavior defames the whole group.

As a wealthy Christian who opened his home to a local church gathering (probably thirty-to-forty persons) and to traveling visitors, Philemon would have been honored as a patron of the community. He probably provided material resources for other needs, such as the communal meal, as well. Paul's lavish praise of the love that Philemon shows fellow Christians undoubtedly includes such activities even though we do not know exactly to what "the hearts of the saints have been refreshed" (verse 7) alludes. If Philemon had the letter read in the assembly as the address suggests, we can imagine looks or gestures of approval from the members of the congregation. Faith is evident in the good that love does (verse 6). Paul also says that he has heard of Philemon's reputation for love of the saints (verse 4). Did Onesimus perhaps contribute to that report about his master?

THANKSGIVING FOR A CHRISTIAN

• "Get a card. It's easier." My ten-year-old niece had already figured out the solution to the pain of writing the obligatory thank-you note. "Will you make one if I get the stuff?" I replied. She agreed. How do thank-you notes work in your family?

• Can you imagine being required to begin every letter with some expression of thanks for the person to whom you are writing?

• What would it feel like to get a letter that began, "I always thank God for your . . . ."?

• Review Philemon 4-7. Philemon is going to get an extra honor from this thanksgiving. It will be read to the whole church that meets in his house. List the phrases that Paul uses in giving thanks for Philemon's faith. Which ones would you most like to have said about you?

• The early Christians had no public buildings; so they always met in the houses of wealthier members of the group, which probably limited the group to about forty persons. What size is your church?

• When you walk into church on Sunday morning, how many faces do you seek out? How many persons do you ask about family issues, such as their health or an update on the children or grandchildren or about planning something for the church?

• A sociologist friend says that he thinks most active Christians interact with thirty-to-forty people in the congregation—just the size of an early Christian house church. Test out his theory. See how you score on the "house church scale."

A New Family Member
Read Philemon 8-16

Enough with the praise. Paul gets down to business by asserting that he will not command, though he could (verse 8). Instead, he will appeal to the love for which Philemon is already well-known (verse 9a). Unlike other writers, who interceded for slaves with their masters, Paul does not refer to the punishment that a master had the right to inflict on a slave who had made off with some of his property (verse 18) or to Paul's own precarious legal situation if he had harbored Onesimus without Philemon's consent. Instead, Paul presents the situation as an opportunity for Philemon to demonstrate his well-known love for fellow Christians (verse 14). Can this love bridge the gulf between master and a less than satisfactory slave? Much depends upon the success of Paul's appeal.

Ancient rhetoric included persuasion by appeal to the emotions of an audience. Paul uses the image of the house church as family to make the case that the Onesimus who returns as a baptized Christian is not the same person who left Colossae. Instead, he is the "child" of an aged, imprisoned father: Paul (verse 10). Although he bears a common slave name (a pun on the Greek for "useful"), Onesimus the Christian can now live up to that name. How? He can represent Philemon by assisting the imprisoned apostle (verse 13), a role fulfilled by Epaphroditus for the Philippian church (Philippians 4:10-20).

Paul carries the substitution even further. Remember the praise for refreshing the hearts (Greek *splanchna*, "guts") of the saints (Philemon 7)? Now Onesimus is presented to Philemon as Paul's "heart" (*splanchna*, verse 12). Notice how Paul has abased himself. He is an old man, imprisoned, pleading for a child born of his chains (verse 10) before a powerful patron.

This emotional transference is so powerful that many readers think Paul hopes for more than he says. Perhaps Philemon will give Onesimus his freedom and send him back to the apostle. If not, there is always the face-saving option provided in verses 15-16. Philemon can treat the breach not as a legal problem of a runaway slave, but as an example of God's providence. As a Christian, Onesimus is to be received as a valued member of both Philemon's physical household and of the church community that gathers in his house.

As a Christian, Onesimus is no longer a "slave" but a "beloved brother." Unlike the status of slave, which can be changed for the worse by sale or harsh punishment and for the better by manumission, the relationship between Christians is forever (verse 16). How effective is the argument? Readers often come to different conclusions. But a "beloved brother" named Onesimus is sent back to Colossae by Paul in Colossians 4:9. If he were the same man, Paul's confidence in the transforming power of Christian faith was not misplaced.

A NEW FAMILY MEMBER

• "That man will never do any good for anyone," a friend sitting next to me in church said, nodding in the direction of an unfamiliar man in his fifties dressed in an old, freshly pressed suit and sneakers. Recently released from prison, he was seated with his parents, though a gap in the pew suggested a family less than pleased at being reunited. Why bring up such an example? It may be the closest thing in our experience to what people thought when Onesimus walked into the church meeting in his master's house. How do you think Onesimus was seated or standing in relation to the rest of the congregation?

• You might like to look at the problem of discrimination in a house church in James 2:1-13.

• No one welcomed the ex-convict to our church. His parents, wife, and children remain active members of the community, which rebuilt their house when it was about to be condemned. Look at what Paul asks Philemon and the church in his house to do. Review Philemon 8-16.

• The "you" in this section of the letter is second person singular, speaking to Philemon; but the address suggests that the letter would have been read to the church. If you were in the congregation, would you be looking for signs of discomfort on the face of Philemon? Or would you be sneaking a glance at Onesimus?

• How would you expect Onesimus to look as this section of the letter is being read?

• Now look at the rhetorical strategy Paul used in the appeal. If you did not know that Onesimus had committed a crime against his master, what kind of person would you expect him to be?

• Some people feel that Paul went too far in presenting himself as an old, chained prisoner sending back his beloved child and support. They think that Paul was shamelessly manipulating the emotions of the audience. Do you agree? If so, why?
• Other people defend Paul's rhetoric. They point out that the Christian house church was a new kind of family. Onesimus should be given a chance to belong as a valued member of the family. Would you agree with this view? Explain.

Housekeeping Details
Read Philemon 17-22

Private letters often end with lists of practical details that need attention, along with some comment about the sender's future plans. So, too, here. Paul leaves rhetoric behind. If Philemon wishes to continue to be counted as a "fellow worker" in Paul's mission ("consider me your partner," Philemon 17), then he has to treat Onesimus as he would treat Paul. But there is some issue of justice behind the conflict; that is, Onesimus may have made off with some of Philemon's property (verse 18). How much, and for what reason, we do not know. Paul agrees to go surety for Onesimus' pilfering, if any (verse 18), and authenticates the promise by writing the conclusion to the letter in his own hand (verse 19; compare Galatians 6:11).

Does Paul expect Philemon to present him with a big bill? It does not seem so. Paul gently reminds Philemon that he owes the Christian life of which he is so proud to the apostle (Philemon 19b). So Paul repeats both the plea and his confidence in Philemon, writing now in his own hand (verses 20-21). Then, just at the end, Paul adds a spot of good news: Get the guest room ready. Paul expects his case to be disposed of favorably in a short time (verse 22).

The Roman road from Ephesus to Colossae followed the Meander and Lycus (modern Ürüksu) rivers to Laodicea and then to Colossae, 120 miles away. On foot, the journey would take about 10 days.

HOUSEKEEPING DETAILS

• The previous section opened with Paul laying aside the authority to command (Philemon 8). How do you relate to the shift in tone in verse 17? Has Paul taken off the mask and decided to command? Or is he just providing the expected letter ending, listing details that need to be attended to?

• As was customary, Paul had dictated to a scribe; but he wrote the last bit in his own hand (verse 19). Suppose we had found the autograph of Paul? What do you think the signature would bring at auction?

• Perhaps the best surprise is at the end. Paul hopes to visit soon (verse 22). How would you prepare to receive him?

Hardly Alone
Read Philemon 23-25

The standard letter conclusion, "farewell," is modified in Pauline correspondence. As with the greeting, it takes the form of a blessing (verse 25). Others with ties to the recipients of the letter often ask to have their greetings included at the end. How well these individuals were known to Onesimus is unclear. They are identified with reference to their place in the Pauline mission. Epaphras, apparently the missionary who had carried the gospel to Colossae (Colossians 1:7; 4:12-13), is now in prison with Paul.

The others are associates in Paul's missionary work. They all appear as active in or passing through this region of the Lycus valley in Colossians 4:7-17. Indeed, their faith and energy will be needed to carry Christianity to the next generation. The chained prisoner who signs off in Colossians 4:18 is not expecting release. Paul's moving appeal in the body of the letter narrowed our gaze to an old man pleading for the son who is his only support in life. Even Paul's beloved Timothy (verse 1) is out of the picture. So it comes as something of a shock to be reminded that Paul was not alone. His activities had established many such house church families, and his faithful fellow workers included many men and women whose names never even appear in a greeting list. We owe our faith to them as much as to the apostle.

HARDLY ALONE

• Using a Bible dictionary, look up the names of those people mentioned in Philemon 23-25. What else can we learn about them?
• Do you feel, or have you ever felt, completely alone? Did you have a church family at that time? Is this a family that can be cultivated? If not, why do you feel that way (and why do you stay)?

IN CLOSING

• Consider the ways in which persons are enslaved in our society (by addictive behaviors, by economic difficulties, by dysfunctional relationships, and so on).
• Turn over to God the issues, behaviors, and beliefs that keep you from being free. Offer prayers that the gospel will be a liberating influence in their lives and in yours.

II NEW AGE RELIGION

An Apostle's Voice
Read Colossians 1:18

Colossians begins as Paul's letters usually do with the address and greeting (Colossians 1:1-2), followed by a report of the apostle's thanksgiving prayer for the recipients (1:3-8). Notice the emphasis on the special Christian virtues: "faith in Christ Jesus," "love for all the saints," and "hope laid up in heaven" (1:4-5). Since Paul expands on hope as the fruit of the gospel, we can expect to hear more about Christian hope in the body of the letter. In Chapter 2, we will see that some false teachers had created a strange religious mix of Christian faith, ascetic practices, and mystic journeys into the heavenly regions. In Chapter 3, the apostle gives practical advice for leading a Christian life with the mind set on "the things that are above" (3:2). That is real new age religion, not a fancy-sounding spirituality stew.

Who are these Christians? They live in Colossae, a city in southwestern Asia Minor on the river Lycus some 120 miles from the coastal city of Ephesus, a center of Paul's missionary work for almost three years (Acts 19:8-10). Paul did not bring the gospel to Colossae. He gives credit to an associate named Epaphras, who also preached in the neighboring cities of Hieropolis and Laodicea (Colossians 4:12-13).

Epaphras has told Paul about the Christians at Colossae. According to Philemon 23, Epaphras had been imprisoned along with Paul, presumably for preaching the gospel, though he does not seem to be in jail when Colossians is written. Some scholars think that Epaphras had gone to Ephesus to enlist Paul's aid in dealing with the strange new religious teaching in Colossae and was detained for questioning when he began preaching the gospel.

Others wonder if Colossians refers to the same imprisonment that Paul mentioned in his letter to Philemon. Perhaps the prisoner here is in Roman custody. There are some unusual turns of phrase in Colossians that make others question Paul's authorship. Paul may have been dead already or lost on the journey to Rome. A close personal associate like Timothy, the co-sender, could have sent a letter in Paul's name to stem the tide of false teaching. Since the evidence for authorship remains inconclusive, we will speak of Paul as the voice behind the teaching of Colossians even if an associate crafted its wording.

AN APOSTLE'S VOICE

• Look at a map of Paul's missionary journeys in an atlas or in your study Bible. Find Ephesus (near present-day Turkey) and Colossae.

• Imagine walking back and forth on those roads as Paul and other early Christians had to. It was much like the first settlers moving west in our country. Now add to your mental map the ups and downs of the hills, the miles of isolated roads without settlements, and the dangers of robbers. Would you stay home instead?

• Paul speaks of Christian hope "bearing fruit and growing in the whole world" (1:6). Look at a map of Roman roads. Imagine faith spreading out from cities like Ephesus and Corinth along those roads.

• Read Colossians 1:3-8. How are faith, love, and hope related to Christian experience?

• Paul has not yet visited Colossae, but he is confident that the Colossians have love for him. How does he know this?

Spiritual Wisdom
Read Colossians 1:9-23

We might expect Paul to get down to business; but the "for this reason" leads into another prayer report (Colossians 1:9-14), a fragment or paraphrase of a hymn to Christ the Creator and Redeemer (1:15-20) and its application to the Colossian converts (1:21-23). This new prayer sharpens the categories of faith and hope by emphasizing the need for Christians to develop "knowledge of God's will" and "spiritual wisdom and understanding" (1:9). This knowledge is not simple book learning. It is crucial to living the Christian life to which God calls us (1:10). Bearing fruit and growing in knowledge of God point out that Christian life is not a set of fixed laws for a people and a place. It requires growth in discerning what God's will is. (Paul chided the Christians at Corinth when their divisive conduct showed a lack of maturity; see 1 Corinthians 3:1-9). A life rooted in Christ has patience and strength to endure difficulty, suffering, or persecution, not in a spirit of sadness, but joyfully thanking God for salvation (Colossians 1:11-12).

What makes this life of a Christian different from the life of a pious Jew who finds God's love and wisdom in living by Torah ("Happy are we, O Israel, / because we know what is pleasing to God" [Baruch 4:4, Apocrypha])? Or what makes it different from the virtuous life of a person schooled in the philosophical teaching of Plato, Aristotle, or the Stoics? Many features of a just and noble life are shared. But Christians tell a special story of salvation that is the basis for their way of life. Paul now recalls that story.

Before they heard the gospel, the Colossians were neither pious Jews nor noble philosophers. They may have prayed to gods, goddesses, and various local spirits for good crops, health, a child, good luck, or to ward off evil; and they may have participated in festivals and rites. But such religion did not provide a spur to morality. It did not point devotees toward God.

Paul reminds them what it was like to be without God. It meant being in darkness, burdened with sins, even perhaps being hostile to God or to what is good (Colossians 1:12-13, 21-23). But all that is past. As long as the Colossians are faithful, they have a terrific hope, an angelic destiny with God. The gospel great news is for "every creature under heaven" (1:23). Sinfulness destroys more than individuals. It infects everything in creation (compare Romans 8:18-25).

This depiction of the Christian experience of conversion frames the central gem of this section, a hymn to Christ as image and creative power of God (Colossians 1:15-17) and as redeemer whose death and resurrection brought the church into being (1:18-20). The first set of phrases identifying Christ as the sustaining creative power in all things is more formulaic than those dealing with redemption. Some scholars think that Paul may have added the second strophe to a pre-formed tradition that identified Christ with God's preexistent wisdom. The original wisdom theology celebrated God's powerful ordering visible in the created universe (compare Proverbs 8:22-31; Wisdom of Solomon 7:22–8:1, Apocrypha).

Redemption, by contrast, presupposes a universe broken apart from God by sin. Some scholars think that the creation stanza originally concluded with the phrase "and he is the head of the body the church" (Colossians 1:18a). They think this because the relative clause "he is the beginning, the firstborn from the dead" (1:18b) parallels "he is the image of the invisible God, firstborn of all creation" (1:15).

But "the church" may not have been in the original version of verse 18a. When Paul uses the word *church*, he refers to local gatherings of Christians, not to a cosmic or heavenly entity. Similarly, the church as "body of Christ" in 1 Corinthians 12:12-25 and Romans 12:4-5 uses the civic metaphor of a community as a body to appeal for communal unity in Christ. When the two-part hymn was composed, the image of "body" shifted from the cosmos pervaded by God's wisdom or reason to the church united with its head, Christ.

Aren't those details best left to scholars and theologians? Why should ordinary Christians care? Today, stories about the human Jesus are big sellers; news magazines and TV networks exploit them shamelessly—Jesus as miracle worker, as agrarian peasant, as liberal rabbi, as defender of the marginal and dispossessed, as prophetic visionary of a new humanity, and so on. But the most important fact about Jesus cannot be stated in those terms.

Philosophers, prophets, and faithful, pious Jews, as well as the champions of the oppressed, were martyred before Jesus and continue to be martyred after him. Their deaths may focus attention on the injustice that killed them, but they do not reconcile humanity to God. As they experienced the crucified and risen Jesus, exalted as Lord, Christians realized that Jesus was not just an extraordinary man. Somehow in Jesus, God was at work. This hymn shows that at a very early stage, the preexistent Wisdom of God provided a clue. The glorious female presence of God (Wisdom) that pervades the universe and inhabits the souls of the wise is uniquely attached to Jesus.

The second stanza shows how the Wisdom imagery provides a cosmic dimension to the church. The church is not the limited, historical, and sociological groupings of believers. It is that divine fullness of God that dwells in the risen Christ, the head of the body (Colossians 1:19).

Since Wisdom pervades and sustains creation, the gospel must be addressed to creation as well. All things are reconciled to God in Christ. As we look out on our expanding cosmos, this vision carries a special message. God and Christ are not confined to our planet, solar system, or galaxy. If we were to meet "alien intelligences" out there, then the gospel would be for them too. Sometimes people think that Jesus could not be Savior elsewhere in the universe because he did not live there. Not so. Redemption through the cross belongs to all God's creation.

SPIRITUAL WISDOM

• Think about who is on the prayer list at your church and why. Then read Colossians 1:9-14 and turn it into a prayer list for the church. Any surprises?

• Paul spends a lot of time on knowledge, understanding, and spiritual wisdom. What is the role of understanding in Christian faith?

• Recall experiences of getting a new hymnal or of learning new hymns. Then read Colossians 1:15-20, which in its time was based on a new, Christian hymn (of course, there were no "old" hymns to Christ in A.D. 60). It has two parts: Christ as God's power working in creation and Christ as God's power in our redemption through the cross.

• How does this hymn influence your understanding of God and Jesus Christ?

• What is your favorite creation hymn? What is your favorite cross hymn?

• Do your favorite hymns have any themes in common with this hymn?

• Paul comes back to the theme of faith and hope as he applies the hymn to his readers. His purpose is to make their faith firm. What role do hymns play in building up your faith?

• What hymn do you find yourself humming when the going gets rough?

• Sing or say together one of these favorites. How does the music, in addition to the words, inspire or influence your faith?

Suffering for the Gentiles
Read Colossians 1:24-29

Taking our image of salvation out to the edges of the universe seems grand indeed. In the next chapter we will see that the "new age" spirituality of the Colossians followed that path as well. But cosmic visions risk losing the cross. Early on Holy Thursday morning, I was having breakfast in a local coffee shop. A familiar drifter, a struggling alcoholic most often found asleep in an armchair at Barnes & Noble, came in with a friend who is mentally retarded. They were discussing baseball and lunch. He remarked, "Tomorrow's Friday. I should have tuna fish — if I can remember. At least tomorrow. It's the big one. The day the Lord hung." Busy at church all day on Good Friday, I did not see him; so I do not know how it worked out. But he had the right idea. It was a big day. The Lord "hung" for him. He needed to respond.

Paul uses his own example to call the reader back to earth in this section. Being a servant of the gospel is not a quick trip to honor, power, recognition, or glory. It is a chance to suffer with a mission. Paul's mission is to spread the gospel to the "big world," the Gentiles of the Roman Empire, not to remain within the confines of his familiar and beloved Jewish tradition (see Galatians 1:11-24). He can take pride in the fact that many others were spurred on by his efforts to establish the gospel in places he had not visited, such as Colossae.

Paul speaks of all this as a *mystery*, a special term used among Jews for God's hidden plan to bring human history to a climax. Before he knew Jesus, Paul had thought that God's plan was to create a remnant, a holy people from among the Jews, and to condemn the rest as sinners.

When Paul had the vision of the risen Lord that changed his life, he realized that God had a bigger, grander plan. God's plan was to reconcile humanity, to bring everyone together as God's people (Colossians 1:25-27).

A big job for a big apostle! And it had an extraordinary price. Paul could have been an honored, esteemed rabbi in his old age. Instead, he was a prisoner in Roman custody. His physical health was wrecked by years of travel and labor at a trade. His body bore the actual marks of punishments he received when both Jewish and civic authorities tried to stop him from preaching (see Galatians 6:17). Did he ever sit back and ask, "Was the sacrifice worth it?" This section gives us his answer to such a question: a vigorous yes! Even as an old man, the vision of bringing people who had never heard of God to Christ and helping them mature in faith inspired enthusiasm (Colossians 1:28-29).

As for the sufferings, Paul makes an extraordinary statement: "In my flesh I am completing what is lacking in Christ's afflictions for the sake of his body, the church" (Colossians 1:24). Paul does not mean that the cross was insufficient to redeem all creation. What he seems to mean is better put in some of his other letters, namely that Christians have to see the suffering God in the devotion and suffering of the apostle. "Be imitators of me, as I am of Christ," he told the Corinthians (1 Corinthians 11:1). Ancient moralists placed a premium on learning by example. Christians cannot learn how to be disciples of the crucified and risen Lord if they do not see Christ in the apostle.

SUFFERING FOR THE GENTILES

• "I've never understood how God could ask his Son to die on a cross," a member of our senior citizens Bible study protested with an edge of anger in her voice. What makes suffering worth it?

• Jesus was not ordered to die; he chose death for sinners. Read Colossians 1:20-23. What do you think of when you hear the words "making peace through the blood of his cross" (1:20)?

• Do you believe Paul when he claimed to be rejoicing in his sufferings? What made suffering to spread the gospel worth it for Paul? What suffering would you be willing to endure for the sake of the gospel?

• "My mind is fine; but my body's out there doing its own thing, breaking down," another senior remarked. Better that than the other way around, they all agreed. Would you?

• By the time Paul wrote Colossians, he had lots of reasons to feel old and broken down. He was old by ancient standards; he had been subjected to a very hard life, including prison. Did Paul regret the life he had led? Do you? If you could change one thing about your life of faith, what would it be? Why?

• Ancient moralists said that the best way to learn virtue was to see it embodied in a wise person. How does Paul embody what it means to be a disciple of Christ? What challenges does his example present for us today?

IN CLOSING

• Review the main themes of Colossians 1: Paul's rejoicing for the Christians in Colossae, the supremacy of Christ, and Paul's willingness to suffer for Christ.

• Pray for the wisdom to see God at work in the world and for the courage to be used by God for this work. Celebrate the gift of the current and previous "saints" with whom you labor for Christ.

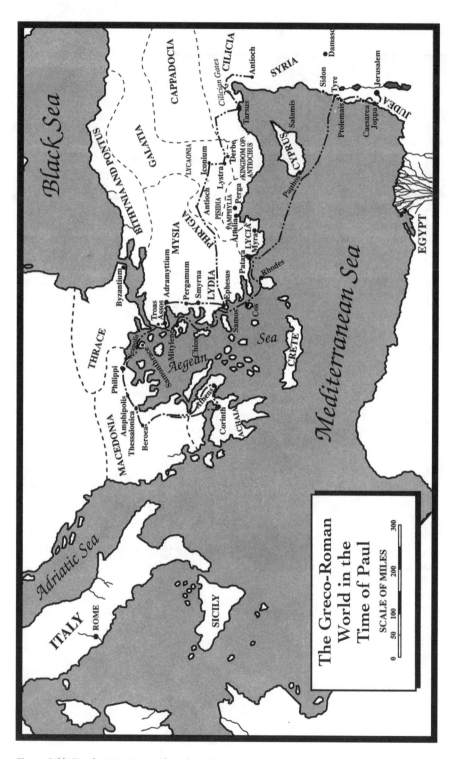

The Greco-Roman World in the Time of Paul

SCALE OF MILES

0   50 100   200   300

From *Bible Teacher Kit,* © 1994 by Abingdon Press

III TRUE LIFE IN CHRIST

Christ Is the Mystery
Read Colossians 2:1-7

The phrase, "I want you to know" (Colossians 2:1), usually means that the author of a letter is getting down to business. By the rules of ancient rhetoric, that makes all of Colossians 1 an inspiring warm-up. Paul wants to make sure that the audience is firmly on his side. The translation, "I am struggling" (2:1), does not convey the image that Paul intends. The Greek word *agon* does mean "a struggle or fight," but it also refers to an athletic contest or a race. Paul introduced this athletic imagery in Colossians 1:29. The energy with which he is engaging in the "athletic struggles" for the gospel is being supplied by God—not by "sports" food or drinks! Paul often used athletic images for his ministry, since the "games," such as boxing, wrestling, and running, were familiar entertainment in Greco-Roman cities (see 1 Corinthians 9:25). Paul is no weekend warrior. He engages in hard training to ensure the success of his ministry.

Along with Colossae, Paul includes another church in the Lycus valley, Laodicea, ten miles away. Laodicea was a wealthy city. When an earthquake hit the region around A.D. 60, the Laodiceans were able to rebuild without outside aid (Tacitus, *Annals*; 14:27). Perhaps Colossae never recovered from that disaster, since Laodicea is the only one of these two cities mentioned in Revelation (3:14-22).

Though none of these Christians has ever met him, Paul wants them to think of him as their "Olympic champion." Why? So that they will continue to live the Christian life as Paul and his associates have taught it to them. There is a danger out there: other, fancier religious preachers, gurus, and teachers. Paul knows that marketing can sell anything. Be cautious, he warns. "Sounds good" (the "plausible arguments" of Colossians 2:4) is not the same thing as a strong Christian life.

People are just as confused today. They often say, "I don't belong to a church, but I'm a very spiritual person." Asked what that means, sometimes it means that they are devoted to some new age book like *A Course in Miracles* or have read all the volumes of *Chicken Soup for "X"* or *Conversations With God*. Not good enough. Paul is right. Religion and an active spirituality mean practice, training, and being part of the church.

CHRIST IS THE MYSTERY

• There is a whole genre of "sweating athlete" commercials aimed at persuading us to buy "product X." How do you react to those ads? Do you respond differently when the central figure is a red, white, and blue-clad Olympian rather than a rich superstar? If so, why?

• What about Paul casting himself as the star of a "power athlete" commercial? Since his readers had never seen him, they must have made up a picture to go with his words. How do you think they would have described Paul as their local hero?

• How do you imagine Paul?

• Read Colossians 2:1-7. List all the benefits that Paul wants his audience to have.

• How often does Paul use words that imply strength and firmness?

• Why, do you think, does Paul link having a firm faith with wisdom and knowledge?

• TV personalities often complain that people treat them like their TV characters or that perfect strangers will act like they are friends just because they have seen that personality on TV. In this passage, Paul wants his readers to feel that they know him even though they have never met. How does he convey that message?
• How does the faith of other Christians encourage the apostle in his ministry?

Facing Down the Competition
Read Colossians 2:8-19

Paul opens with a strong warning. He refers to the opposition as powerful speakers. They know how to manipulate human hopes using a language that appears high sounding or expert (2:8). Philosophy in ancient society covered a much broader range than it does today. Even a "new age" phenomenon like Scientology that sells by appearing "scientific" would come under this warning. Paul knows that these competing philosophies have power over people. He explains it by referring to the "elemental spirits of the universe" (2:8).

The expression is deliberately vague. The Greek word *stoicheia* usually means the elemental substances out of which the universe is made (see Wisdom of Solomon 7:17, Apocrypha). But it also had been expanded in popular imagination; that is, the "elements" were connected with gods or spirits. In some cases, this identification was attached to astrology. The powers connected to the signs of the zodiac and the planets were responsible for human destiny. Thus Paul can characterize all the superstitious and religious practices of pagans as being in servitude to the "elemental powers" (Colossians 2:20; also Galatians 4:3, 9). Of course, Jews also wondered what powers were linked to the stars. Angels were usually given the job.

There is no need to turn to such powers, whether conceived as pagan deities or even as angels. Through baptism Christians are taken up into the kingdom of the one who governs them all (Colossians 2:10). The expression "ruler and authority" appears to be equivalent to "elemental spirits." If one treats these authorities as angels who participate in governing God's creation, then Christ as God's creating Wisdom must be their superior. Early Christians recognized the enthronement of Christ at his resurrection as exaltation above the angels. (See the hymn that Paul quotes in Philippians 2:6-11 and a similar use of Wisdom tradition in Hebrews 1:2-4.) Some scholars have set out Colossians 2:9-12 in short parallel lines as a hymn or poem celebrating redemption. Christ, who possesses all the fullness of deity, brings it to bear on the reality of believers.

The ritual of baptism is described as spiritual circumcision, burial with Christ and resurrection with him (2:11-12). This complex of symbols played an important role in Paul's instruction of Gentiles. He appeals to it in contexts where he must defend the inclusion of Gentiles as God's people even though they did not adopt a Jewish way of life. Spiritual circumcision follows God's will from the heart. A righteous Gentile puts lax and disobedient Jews to shame (Romans 2:10-16, 25-29). Dying with Christ to sin in baptism is not a license to do as one pleases. Christians should recognize rising with Christ as the call to a life of holiness (Romans 6:1-11).

Is the new religious preaching that threatens the Lycus valley a form of Jewish propaganda aimed at Gentile Christians? Some have thought so. But there are elements in this response that suggest that the claim is not to what might be considered ordinary Jewish practices. Therefore, a more common view is that the false religion was some-

thing that we might call a "new age" Judaism. It appealed
to the Jewish Scriptures but also to astrology and mystical
traditions. This distortion would be very confusing indeed.
It might seem to be another form of what the Colossians
came to believe when they rejected paganism. Note the
dramatic shift in image in Colossians 2:14-15. Christ is
pictured like a Roman conqueror. He rips up the record of
sins or debts that stood against pagans. Then he defeats
the cosmic powers. They are not just assistants. They are
conquered enemies put on display in the emperor's tri-
umphal procession.

Verses 16-19 provide a few more clues about what these
new age religious teachers were up to. They had special
rules about food and drink, perhaps Jewish kosher laws
combined with other food taboos such as those among
Pythagorean philosophical groups. Today we can point to
food taboos that go beyond health concerns. These groups
also had an elaborate calendar of festival days, including
Jewish sabbaths (verse 16). So far, one might agree that this
is just an attempt to make Gentile Christians more Jewish.

But verse 18 introduces a new twist. This "new age"
Judaism goes in for "self-abasement," that is, ascetic practices like strict fasting combined with long prayers. It seeks
visions and apparently claims that those who have a vision
actually experience heavenly worship. "Worship of angels"
need not mean that devotees worshiped angels instead of
God. It could mean worshiping along with the angelic
hosts. When Paul speaks of "putting off the body of the
flesh" in spiritual circumcision (2:11), he means the end to
the physical distinctions between persons, especially Jew
and Gentile (compare Galatians 3:26-28). But the visionaries probably claimed to "put off the flesh" through fasting
and prayer so that the soul could ascend into the heavens.

Visionaries may have claimed to replicate the experiences of Isaiah (6:1-3), Daniel (7:9-10), or Enoch (1 Enoch 14:18-23, Pseudepigrapha; for fasting in a posture of humility as the prior condition to revelation, see 2 Esdras 5:13; 6:35, Apocrypha). The phrase that follows "worship of angels" (Colossians 2:18), if translated literally, reads "which [things] he had seen upon entering," that is, upon entering the heavenly regions. The "he" is the hypothetical devotee of this new age mysticism. The NRSV says, "dwelling on visions," which indicates what the false teachers were interested in, but not the destination they claimed to have reached. What is the downside of this new form of Judaism? Paul reaches a severe conclusion: nothing less than being cut off from the real source of heavenly life, Christ (Colossians 2:19).

FACING DOWN THE COMPETITION

• List all the traits of the empty and deceitful teaching that Paul mentions in Colossians 2:8-19. How many of them can you find a parallel for today? What makes these beliefs or practices "empty"? What is the deceit that is involved in them?

• How does Paul use images of Christ as God's cosmic Wisdom and power to show readers that they do not have to go on looking for spirituality outside the faith that they received when they were baptized?

• We know how easily people can do real harm to themselves by trying to remold their bodies. Paul makes references to "body" in almost every verse. Make two lists: references to the "body of Christ," a true Christian life, and references to what the competition requires.

• Why do the bodily practices of a false religion lead to a false religious pride, becoming "puffed up" (verse 18)?

• Since the "elemental spirits of the universe" were thought to govern the planets, Paul's argument against their power over baptized Christians applies to belief in astrology. Do you know Christians who say they believe in astrology? What would Paul tell them?

• Why does belief in astrology or in some new age "add-on" show that a Christian lacks faith in the salvation received from Christ?

Useless Religion
Read Colossians 2:20-23

The final warning against believing such new teachings treats the rules for ascetic practice and holiness as no better than what superstitious pagans do. These practices are made up by human beings and could make an individual seem very pious. The reasons given make it seem like religious wisdom. (The NRSV has translated the Greek *logos*, "word or reason," as "appearance.") But these practices do not accomplish the goal of Christian life, changing what is in a person's heart, the topic to be treated in the next section of the letter (3:1–4:6).

Paul wraps up the complex play on images of body and flesh by saying that the ascetic religious practices are without value for "checking self-indulgence," that is, for gratification of the flesh (2:23). What does he mean? The NRSV concludes that he means that the asceticism does not curb a person's tendency to self-indulgence. Perhaps. But the overall thrust of the sentence appears to be that the new age teachers and their manipulations of "the flesh" for the sake of fancy religious experience are engaging in a kind of fleshly indulgence (compare 1 Corinthians 13:3). Despite the appearance of advanced spirituality, this new religious movement cannot bring Christians any closer to God than their baptism into Christ already has done.

USELESS RELIGION

• Many Christians today assume that religion should not have rules that govern food, handling certain objects, ritual purification, and the like. These Christians are surprised to see Orthodox Jews, Muslims, Hindus, Buddhists, and devotees of other religious traditions engaging in practices that regulate all these matters. Seen from the other side, Christians do not appear very religious. Do you have any special practices or rituals that are part of your daily life as a Christian?

• When Christians agreed that non-Jewish converts did not have to adopt the Jewish way of life (see Galatians 2:1-14), they shed the special forms of practice that marked someone as Jewish. How does Paul make the case for Christians as holy and spiritual persons even though they lack such physical, bodily practices?

• Think about what "useless religion" means to you. If Christian teaching or worship is false, misleading, or useless, what does that say about the community of faith that spawns or allows it?

• Paul makes two charges against a system of religious rules that manipulates the body: These rules can be equivalent to pagan superstition, and they can be a form of self-indulgence. Can you think of examples today that would prove the truth of either of these claims?

• What do you think Paul would say about such crazes as body piercing and elaborate body tattooing? Both activities appear as religious rites in other societies.

IN CLOSING

• Review the main themes of Colossians 2: the fullness of life in Christ, discerning between true and false teaching about Christ, and authentic spiritual worship.

• Close in prayer for Christian teachers and worship leaders to be spiritually renewed and faithfully grounded. Pray for your own understanding of the wonderful mysteries of the faith.

IV GOD'S CHOSEN ONES

New Life in Christ
Read Colossians 3:1-17

A final section of ethical exhortation concludes the body of this letter as it does in most of Paul's letters (see Romans 12–15; Galatians 5–6). It develops the final argument that the holiness in life that Christianity seeks is grounded in baptismal conversion. Claims to lofty religious and mystical experience have no place in evaluating a person's Christian calling. Paul opens with a reminder that baptism has united Christians with their exalted Lord. When the end time comes, they will be found with him (Colossians 3:1-4). There is no need for preliminary reconnaissance expeditions.

Ethical exhortation in the New Testament epistles often employs topics, images, and arguments that were commonplaces of Jewish and Greco-Roman moral teaching. Peculiarly Christian convictions do more to shape the motivation and goal of ethical conduct than the details of specific injunctions. The process of bringing conventional moral insights into a Christian framework is easily seen in this section of Colossians. The opening verses have provided the basis and goal for heeding the instruction that follows. Unlike the case of the teachings of ancient philosophers, human excellence and well-being in this life do not figure as the motive for ethical conduct. Nor, contrary to some later forms of Christian preaching, does the fear of divine punishment. Christians are to focus on the destiny they share with the heavenly Christ (3:2-3).

The language of putting off vices and clothing oneself with virtue is traditional, and so is the use of lists of vices and virtues. Colossians has taken over two such lists. One involves passions (3:5). Its Jewish character emerges at the end when greed is equated with idolatry. The second opens with anger but moves into sins of speech, presumably understood as sources for the anger with which the list opens (3:8b-9).

Clothing provides an occasion to move back to a Christian motivation and symbolizes the new, renewed humanity (3:10). Christians would also remember the new garments they put on after emerging from the waters of baptism. Verse 11 may reflect a commonplace in the baptismal formulary. Distinctions of Jew/Gentile, of ethnic origin, or of social status are not part of the "image of God" in the new creation. Galatians 3:26-28 uses a similar formula to argue against requiring Gentile Christians to adopt a Jewish way of life. That formula included "not male and female," thus suggesting that the gender division of Genesis 2 was not part of the divine image in Genesis 1. Scholars wonder if Paul drew back from that element in the formula after his conflicts with Corinthian women prophets who broke with social conventions (1 Corinthians 11:2-16; 1 Corinthians 12:13 also omits "male and female").

The section on virtues has a similar structure. First Paul writes a list of virtues linked to compassion and humility (Colossians 3:12); then he continues with instructions designed to defuse conflict between persons and to encourage patience, mutual tolerance, and forgiveness (3:13).

Forgiveness of others, a peculiarly Christian motivation, is the proper response to forgiveness received from God. Other injunctions to mutual love, peace, and harmony have been given a similar grounding (3:14-15).

Nor has Paul forgotten about those "new age believers" trying to worship in heaven. Notice how he brings in Christian worship. It includes psalms and other music, perhaps hymns like the fragments quoted in the letter, along with instruction and moral exhortation (3:16). Extraordinary ascetic efforts and visions are not necessary, since God can be thanked in every activity of life (3:17).

NEW LIFE IN CHRIST

• One Sunday a visiting preacher told our congregation, "People spend so much time thinking about this life, about earthly things. They hardly think about life in heaven at all." (We were still talking about that several days later!) Make a list of the earthly things that you think about all day. Then list the heavenly things. Now make the same two lists based on what Paul says in Colossians 3:1-17.

• How do your lists and Paul's list compare? Is there anything from Paul's list that you would like to move over to your personal list?

• At Easter, instead of sweets, we gave the kids assorted small toys, including a night light that was very popular with my 3 ½ -year-old nephew. This change got me thinking: How should we connect Easter, rising to new life, and "being good"? That is where Paul begins this section.

• In the ancient church, adults were baptized at Easter, which symbolized putting away an old life to take on the new life attached to the risen Christ. How do we use these symbols in our churches?

• Can you think of other ways to remind Christians that they are a new creation?

• Remember that Paul thinks of the church as the "body of Christ"— something we are, not something we do. The "body of Christ" also refers to our experiences as a church. How does our church show its Easter renewal?

• "Free speech" versus "hate speech" is a much-debated issue. List all the items in this section that refer to how a Christian should or should not speak.

• Formulate your own description of Christian speech. Apply it to some episode in the news.
• Do you know anyone who always speaks like a Christian? What do you admire about her or his speech?

Household Order
Read Colossians 3:18–4:1

This section employs a pattern of ethical teaching about duties as old as Aristotle (fourth century B.C.). Civic harmony required that the members of households observe the duties appropriate to their station within society. Jews writing in Greek also adopted this form of philosophical teaching. For example, Philo's interpretation of the command to honor one's parents refers to this type of moral instruction (*Decalogue*; 165–167). Does adapting an ethic focused on preserving the harmony and good order of traditional social relationships undermine the equality proclaimed in the baptismal formulae? These formulae suggest that the use of such materials in the later New Testament epistles (also see Ephesians 5:22–6:9; 1 Peter 2:18–3:7; 1 Timothy 2:8-15; 6:1-2; Titus 2:1-10) indicates a Christianity that hopes to settle into the social order rather than to challenge it.

But there is another possibility: the apologetic function that defends such appeals to household order. A fragment from the Neopythagorean philosophical tradition answers suspicions that arose because the philosopher Timaeus (d. 260 B.C.) was known to hold classes for married women (without their husbands) and for boys (without their parents). In his defense, the philosopher is said to have recommended simplicity of life, modesty in conduct, obedience toward husbands and parents, as well as piety toward the gods. The report concludes with the remark,

"This conquest of the women who are usually hard to influence shows the measure of his success with the younger generation."[1] Such a concern could explain the unusual order of the household order in Colossians.

Instead of addressing husbands, parents, and masters as persons responsible for the order and behavior of those under them, Colossians begins each section with the weaker parties: wives, children, and slaves. However, Philo switches the order from the beginning to the end of his remarks for purely rhetorical reasons; so the order in which persons are listed may not indicate that Colossians seeks to ward off the accusation that Christianity disrupts the social order.

This household ethic also recognizes that actions of those who possess power over others can be faulted. Harsh or brutal treatment does not correct. It only creates discord in the household. And in the case of the most abused persons in the ancient household, slaves, their masters will have to reckon with their heavenly master. We misread this ethic if we assume that it gives fathers absolute rights to require unquestioning obedience of everyone in the family, or worse, that wives and children must suffer violence or abusive treatment. That is not a Christian family.

HOUSEHOLD ORDER

• Household order (husbands and wives, parents and children, masters and slaves) was thought to replicate the social order (rulers and subjects, benefactors and recipients). Formulate your own code of behavior for today. What are your categories?

• Ancient society assumed that hierarchy and power were the bases for the categories. Do your categories show the same concerns? How are the modern categories different from the ancient ones?

• Some scholars describe the order involved in such household codes as "love patriarchy," in which the abuses of power are moderated by the concern and gentleness of the superior for his or her inferiors; but the fundamental distribution of power remains unchanged. Critics argue that this system of power relations is antithetical to the gospel. Jesus taught equality in discipleship and service. Do you agree with their critique? Explain.

• How should Christians today relate to the household order sections in the Scripture?

• Can you come up with some rules that should govern the behavior of persons in the categories you listed? Should such rules be peculiar to Christians, or should they apply to all persons? Explain.

Wrapping Up
Read Colossians 4:2-6

Colossians 4:2-6 serves as the rhetorical conclusion to the letter body. The injunction to prayer (4:2; see 1:3, 9; 3:17) asks readers to move from their own concerns to the apostle's mission. Perhaps God can turn even Paul's imprisonment to a renewed opportunity for proclaiming the "mystery," the good news that all people are called into Christ (4:3-4; 1:25-27; 2:2-3). Finally the exhortation to lead a moral Christian life (4:5; 2:6-7) has an apologetic orientation (4:5-6). Even learning the virtues associated with speech (4:6; 3:8) may impress outsiders. Every Christian has a responsibility to provide opportunity for the gospel to be shared. Ordinary Christian lives, exhibiting integrity in actions and speech, are evidence for the truth of the faith.

WRAPPING UP

• Paul creates a neat rhetorical frame around this section: (a) speech inside the Christian community, prayer with thanksgiving (4:2) and (b) speech to outsiders, gracious speech (4:5-6). How are the two ways of speaking related to each other?

• Which form of speech do you find most difficult, thanksgiving prayer or appropriate words to outsiders?

Concluding Greetings
Read Colossians 4:7-18

Ancient letters often conclude with comments about those who carried the letter, even the possibility that the letter-bearer will provide additional information about the sender and his witnesses (4:7-8). The party includes the familiar figure of Onesimus (4:9; see Philemon). As we mentioned in Chapter I, non-Pauline oddities in language suggest that Paul may not have written this letter himself. The "signature" that concludes the epistle (Colossians 4:18; compare Philemon 19; Galatians 6:11) is tacked on to the very end rather than appearing at the conclusion of the prior section. And, even more striking, it is associated with a notice that Paul is in chains. Shackles imply that Paul is suffering a harsh form of imprisonment unlike the looser supervision and access to outsiders permitted earlier (see Philemon). Even the concluding benediction is briefer than Paul's ordinary form. Does this appended scrawl show us the final effort of a suffering prisoner? If so, it emphasizes the pathos of Paul's earlier reflections on apostolic suffering.

Perhaps because Paul's situation was ominous, he provided more detail about the persons named in the final greetings. One could not necessarily anticipate additional letters. Colossians was to be circulated in the house churches of Laodicea as well as in those of Colossae (4:15-16). Most of the names in this list are familiar figures in the Pauline mission. Onesimus, Archippus, Epaphras, Luke, and Demas all appear in Philemon (verses 23-24). They became stable figures in the Pauline churches after Paul's death (2 Timothy 4:9-12, which criticizes Demas for deserting Paul).

This passage is cited to support the tradition that Luke was a physician (Colossians 4:14). *Doctor* was not always a term of honor in antiquity (see Mark 5:26), but this passage appears to use it to designate a person of education and skill in healing. Paul also mentions a prominent woman, Nympha, who heads a house church in the wealthy city of Laodicea. She may owe her wealth to business ventures, perhaps as a widow after the death of her husband. Inscriptions from Pompeii provide examples of such women in this period.

The persons on this list were like the Colossians. They were non-Jews who had been converted by Paul and others who spread the gospel. In a somewhat surprising move, this list of Gentile missionaries is prefaced with the names of several Jewish Christian apostles (Colossians 4:10-11). Mark had been an early associate in Paul's first missionary efforts, based in Antioch (Acts 12:12, 25; 15:38; Philemon 24; 1 Peter 5:12). Aristarchus had been in prison with Paul (Acts 19:29) and had been with him on his missionary journeys (Acts 20:4; 27:2). Jesus Justus is unfamiliar, though Acts mentions two other individuals with Justus as part of a double name (Acts 1:23; 18:7).

Why does Paul highlight the Jewish credentials of these individuals? Perhaps once more, this is a reference to the "new age Judaism" being sold to believers in the Lycus valley. Readers will be relying on the Gentile converts in Paul's mission. So Paul wishes to make it clear to his readers that they stand in a tradition that is the authentic development of its Jewish heritage.

CONCLUDING GREETINGS

• The center of Paul's conclusion (Colossians 4:3-4) reminds us of his mission, as do the greetings that follow (4:7-17). How do we relate to the larger mission of the church?

• Do we wait for special appeals to come in, or do we constantly pray and work for church missions?

• Paul will end the letter with a dramatic reminder of his imprisonment, "remember my chains" (4:18). We know that religious persecution still exists in many parts of the world. When was the last time prisoners of conscience were on your prayer list?

• How can we work together as a church to increase religious freedom and tolerance?

• Amnesty International issued a report in May 2000 that criticized the United States for torture and unjust treatment of prisoners. How do we minister to those who are in prison? How do we minister to those in law enforcement and those who work in prisons?

IN CLOSING

• Summarize your insights about the new life in Christ and the ethical rules that give shape to that life.

• Offer prayer for strength and wisdom to live the life Christ would want you to live and for justice in "household order," whether at home, in business, in church, or elsewhere.

---

[1] From "Neopythagorean Moralists and the New Testament Household Codes," by David L. Balch, in *ANRW* II 26/1; page 382.

Coin of Lystra
© 1986 Biblical Archaeology Society

V CHRIST UNIVERSAL

Claiming a Tradition
Read Ephesians 1:1-2

The final scrawl at the end of Colossians (4:18) shows Paul chained in the severest form of imprisonment. He is no longer permitted the easy access to friends and associates evident in earlier prison letters like Philippians and Philemon. Many scholars think that Colossians was composed by a fellow worker, perhaps the co-sender, Timothy. Although Paul, the prisoner, is depicted as the author of Ephesians, the case against his actual authorship of this letter is almost certain. Ephesians is written in a rhetorical Greek style often using words not characteristic of Paul. Ephesians is modeled on earlier letters of Paul, especially Colossians. Like a student using books for a paper, most of this material has not been copied directly, although subjects, images, and phrases from the earlier letter have been worked in. But the style is different, and no co-sender is mentioned in Ephesians 1. The author identifies himself as a Jewish Christian when he contrasts the group, "we," to which he belongs with "you," the Gentile converts addressed in the letter (2:1-3, 11-14, 19-22). He presents this disjunction as Paul's own voice in the "I" of Ephesians 3:1-13.

We are equally in the dark about where the original letter was sent. We know it as addressed to Ephesus, the capital of the province of Asia Minor and a major center of Paul's missionary activity. But the earliest manuscripts have no address. As you read through the letter, you will also see that it does not speak about problems in a particular local church, as most of Paul's letters do. Some scholars have proposed that Ephesians was written as a general letter, a kind of update on the apostle's teaching for Christians in Asia Minor.

We know that Paul intended to leave his missionary work in Asia Minor and Greece behind when he headed for Jerusalem with the collection (Romans 15:14-33). So he must have felt that the network of associates he had used in founding those churches was able to handle things. They probably had copies of letters Paul had written. It is possible that many of Paul's letters were written from Ephesus—Galatians and First Corinthians during periods of missionary activity or travel through the city; Philippians, Philemon, and perhaps Colossians when Paul was imprisoned there. Second Corinthians may have been written from Macedonia after a period in which Paul had moved his mission activity out of Ephesus (due to hostility? see 2 Corinthians 1:8) to Troas and then crossed from Asia to Europe (2 Corinthians 2:12-13). Some scholars think that Paul himself reedited Romans, First and Second Corinthians, and Galatians to form a mini-collection. Ephesians could have been written by a follower of Paul and attached to that group as a theological summary.

Of course, this scenario is guesswork based on a few clues; but it fits what we know about ancient letter collections. It also reminds us that Paul was no loner. Even though he sometimes expected Jesus to return in glory soon (1 Thessalonians 4:13-18; 1 Corinthians 15:51-52),

Paul established churches for the long haul. Whoever composed Ephesians, evidently a well-educated Jewish Christian, he was acting on Paul's authority. His task was to make sure that churches in western Asia Minor remained faithful to the Pauline tradition. Ephesians 1:15 indicates that the author has in mind readers who were not converted through Paul's personal preaching. The reference to "the holy apostles and prophets" in Ephesians 3:5 suggests that both the author and his audience are looking back on the time of the apostles. Ephesians belongs to a process by which the churches could carry their legacy to the next generation

CLAIMING A TRADITION

• These days most books by big stars or politicians have an "as told to" line identifying the actual writer. Some writers have even gained a reputation for what used to be referred to as "ghost writing." Is that how we should think of the anonymous author of Ephesians?

• Scripture has an established custom of anonymous authors who carry on a tradition that bears the name of a founding figure, for example, Moses as author of the Pentateuch, David as author of the Psalms, or the later Isaiah voices that carried Isaiah of Jerusalem forward into the exilic and post-exilic period in Isaiah 40–66. What difference does it make to the authority of Ephesians if we think of the writer as part of this biblical tradition?

• A third possibility is to invoke a constitutional model and treat Ephesians as a theological development that is in accord with the intent of the Pauline letters. How would you decide whether Ephesians meets this criterion? (Do not take the shortcut of appealing to its presence in the canon.)

• Did you ever have the urge to write a Pauline letter to your church? Shortly before she left for a new assignment, the interim pastor at my brother's church did that. She read it from the pulpit as the sermon—a moving experience for many. (Of course, my professional ear kept noting places where style or content could have been tweaked to be more Pauline; but no one warned her of my visit.)

• Try jotting some notes for a letter to the church. Then try making your letter sound like Paul.

In Praise of Salvation
Read Ephesians 1:3-14

Try reading this section aloud. Did you find it tough? In Greek, verses 3-14 are a single sentence. Most translations divide it up, but it should be printed more like a hymn in shorter verse units. I have a friend who preaches in this style. Rhetorical phrases break up the spiraling train of thought. This way of speaking makes Americans restless. Even though the service in our church ends at the same time regardless of who is preaching, parishioners always complain that his sermons are too long. In antiquity, this style of speaking could win you a prize at the Olympics. No sale in our church!

The sentence begins with an important prayer form, "Blessed be the God . . ." which is familiar in Jewish prayer. It can be a spontaneous word addressed to God (as in Psalm 41:13; 68:35; 89:52). Or it may preface thanksgiving to God for blessings such as deliverance from enemies (as in Exodus 18:10). First Corinthians 10:16 indicates that the verb to bless (Greek, *eulogein*) was used in a eucharistic context. Non-Jewish readers may have been familiar with this prayer language from their liturgical assemblies

The literary form of this section is a eulogy, a speech in praise of someone. Who is the someone? God, the Father, working through the Lord Jesus Christ and the Holy Spirit. The other day I walked into the local coffee shop to find two of the workers arguing about why Christians keep calling God Trinity. "God has to be one. Jesus is just an inspired person," the young woman insisted. The young man, a beginning theology student, was trying to explain "three persons" sharing one nature. Good luck! This eulogy shows how the earliest Christians came at it. They looked at God's plan to work out salvation. That is what this whole complex eulogy is about. It praises God for having had a plan of salvation from the beginning (4:4).

To make the plan work, Jesus cannot just be a human being who loves God and his fellow human beings. Jesus actually has to be God—but God as Son to the Father. To make the plan work, salvation cannot just be a check-off, a pass card to get us into heaven when we die. God actively has to be making believers holy so that they can be joined to God. That is the Holy Spirit at work. It would take a few centuries for Christians to thrash out the philosophical terms for this perception of God—the "three persons, one nature." But the New Testament is full of images of the "Trinity at work."

What is the basic idea in this long piece of rhetoric? God created the universe from the very beginning to unite all things in Christ (1:9-11). God even planned for the faith that has brought the author and his readers to believe in Christ. This predestination is evidence of God's love for us (1:5, 11-13). In the abstract, people can be put off by the idea of predestination. It sounds too much like God deciding in advance who is going to be saved and who is not—as though salvation were programmed (or not) in our genes.

That disconnection happens when we look at salvation as a special reward for the few who manage to get it. Tough luck for the rest! That is not the way Ephesians puts it. Ephesians invites us to wonder, to marvel. How can God take a vast universe and bring it about that we know Jesus Christ?

We can all identify with personal moments of destiny. A couple of years ago, a neighbor in his mid-forties had a massive heart attack. Ordinarily he would have been alone, but through various coincidences his wife was in the room. That was the difference between life and death. We do not talk about it much anymore. Every now and then an experience in church, walking the dog, or watching one's ten-year-old child elicits a "Thank you, God!" In other words, predestination is an appropriate language for the experience of God's blessing and grace.

IN PRAISE OF SALVATION

• What are the "spiritual blessings" for which we say, "Blessed be God"? Make a list of those you consider most important in your life. Now work through Ephesians 1:3-14 listing the spiritual blessings Ephesians speaks of.
• How do they compare with your list? How is God involved in the spiritual blessings on your list? on the list from Ephesians?
• Election or predestination in Ephesians refers to the sense that the course of our life has directed us to knowing and loving God in Christ by the power of the Holy Spirit. How do we find God's action in our lives?
• Make a timeline of your life. Mark the major events or changes as you remember them. Indicate those in which faith played an important role.
• Are there other places where your relationship with God changed, but life went on as usual?
• Suppose you could take everything that has to do with faith in Jesus out of your life. Would it be the same life? What would be missing?

Prayer Report
Read Ephesians 1:15-23

Ephesians picks up Paul's custom of reporting his prayer of thanksgiving for the Christian faith of the addressees (1:15-17; compare Colossians 1:3-4, 9, 18).

Paul expands it with another long sentence; an interces-
sion asks that God give readers the wisdom needed to
understand the plan of salvation as evidence of God's all-
embracing power (Ephesians 1:15-19). God's power is
demonstrated in the risen and exalted Christ, victorious
over all the powers in the universe (1:20-21). Ephesians
attaches an allusion to Psalm 8:6, a text often used to
demonstrate the truth of Christ's exaltation to God's right
hand (see 1 Corinthians 15:27, applied to the end-time
defeat of death, and Hebrews 2:8, the exaltation of Christ
over the angels).

So far, Ephesians reflects common early Christian
themes. But the very end of this long sentence shifts to
a motif from the Pauline tradition as it was developed in
Colossians. The exalted Christ is head of a cosmic body,
the church (see Colossians 1:17-18). Paul had described
the lordship of Christ as the manifestation of God's power
to defeat all enemies, even death, at the end of days (see
1 Corinthians 15:20-28). Ephesians drops the eschatological delay. Christ's triumph is complete, "the fullness of him
who fills all in all" (Ephesians 1:23; compare verse 10).

How does this vision of the church as the cosmic body
of Christ filling the universe reflect on Christian life? In
Colossians, Paul countered the influence of false teachings
about mystic ascent into the heavens by reminding
Christians that they belong to the body of the heavenly
Christ (Colossians 1:24; 2:19). Ephesians will expand this
view of the church in its totality, united with Christ and
embracing the entire cosmos. This vision suggests that
when Ephesians speaks of "glorious inheritance among the
saints" (Ephesians 1:18), the term *saints* or *holy ones* refers
to angelic beings (as in Deuteronomy 33:2; Psalm 89:6-7;

Daniel 8:13) rather than to Christians (as in Ephesians
1:15).

Some scholars think that the insistence upon the power
of Christ's name in Ephesians 1:21 is related to a concrete
situation about which Paul was concerned. Magicians in
antiquity conjured with divine names. Though Christians
might still be tempted to resort to magic in times of crisis
(or fear the use of magic against them), they have nothing
to gain from meddling with such alleged divine powers.

PRAYER REPORT

• The petition asks God to "enlighten the eyes of your hearts" to enable
an understanding of salvation. Why is divine assistance required?

• What makes it difficult for Christians to hold on to the hope of a heavenly destiny?

• If those scholars who see this prayer as a reminder that Christians
should have nothing to do with controlling their destiny through magic
are correct in their interpretation, what modern examples are similar to
this fascination with magic? Where do people place their faith in false
powers to rescue them? How should we respond as Christians?

• The prayer report imagines God's power exalting Christ as head of
a body that fills the whole cosmos. When you look at the latest photo-
graphs of distant galaxies from the Hubble telescope, do you think of
God's awesome power?

• How can Christians expand their images of creation to fit the new
cosmos? (It does not say enough about God's power if we think of the
exalted Christ as "up with the astronauts." As Ephesians suggests,
the body of Christ has to embrace the whole universe.)

Conversion to Christianity
Read Ephesians 2:1-10

Before Ephesians develops the motif of church as body,
it draws author and audience together in a dramatic
description of conversion, from death in sins to life with

the risen Christ (2:1-7). This depiction has mythological elements that could be directed at local fascination with angelic or demonic powers. Humans find themselves trapped by "the ruler of the power of the air" (2:2). The expression "sons of disobedience" (NRSV: "those who are disobedient") or "children of wrath" suggests an apocalyptic scenario. The Essenes described outsiders as "sons of deceit" who followed the spirit of the Angel of Darkness. But Ephesians does not follow this metaphor to an end-time apocalyptic battle between light and dark.

Instead, the ethical reading of disobedience takes over. The trap is not an external, angelic power, but the power of passions (2:3). For those inclined toward astrological speculation, the stars were alleged to dominate by their influence on the body. Horoscopes served as clues to the evils of an individual's character. So the overall impact of the opening verses is to emphasize the problem of sinfulness. Whether through astral worship or some other form of idolatry, this Gentile audience was "dead through the trespasses and sins in which [they] once lived, following the course of this world" (2:1).

Jewish apologists often equated Gentile worship of idols with immorality (see Wisdom of Solomon 2:23-27, Apocrypha; Romans 1:18-32). If the "idols" are interpreted as hostile spiritual powers, then the Gentiles have no chance of pleasing God. But Ephesians shifts from "you" (plural) to "we" in 1:3; sinful alienation from God is attributed to Jew and non-Jew alike (see Romans 2). All are "dead" if they are not right with God. But there is hope.

The rest of this section (Ephesians 2:6-10) celebrates the grace that all Christians experience in Christ. "Rich in mercy" and "love" (2:4) connect the characterization of

God in the eulogy (1:5-8) and prayer report (1:18) with "his [God's] right hand in the heavenly places"—the exaltation of Christ in 1:20-23. An apocalyptic scenario would have believers under siege from the powers of darkness (as in 6:11). But here, the transfer from one region or power to the other is complete. Believers do not have to walk in fear of hostile powers.

Ephesians picks up the language of predestination (2:10) to orient readers toward the future. God, who knows each person's election, also has a purpose in mind: "good works." Whatever empowers sin, the saving power of God is stronger. Nor is this experience simply an individual one, such as in the stories of persons in a recovery group. Ephesians insists on a cosmic perspective. The community of persons who have been freed from sin serves as evidence of God's goodness and kindness in the universe (2:7).

CONVERSION TO CHRISTIANITY

• In the ancient church, most Christians were converts, though Ephesians knows of children growing up in believing families (6:1-4). For them the language of conversion as rescue, being delivered from a life of sin or enslavement to passions, referred to an actual turning point in their life. How do Christians who have grown up in the church experience a conversion to Jesus? Or is conversion language only for those who really have found God after living in unbelief or sin?

• Take a look at the interesting shift between "you" (the Gentile Christian audience) and "we" in Ephesians 2:1-10. The tricky part is figuring out when "us" or "we" means the author of Ephesians and other Jewish Christians as opposed to "you" Gentiles and when it means the author and the audience. What distinctions are made here? Are such distinctions important to maintain now? Explain.

• Read the Jewish views of the immorality of non-Jews in Romans 1:18-32 and in Wisdom of Solomon 12:23-27 if your Bible has an Apocrypha. Compare it with the "you" statements in Ephesians 2:1-10.

• How does the author of Ephesians include the experiences of Jewish Christians in the pattern of conversion in verse 3? Compare this move with Paul's way of bringing the Jew under sin in Romans 2:1–3:20.

• How has Ephesians generalized the more detailed argument given by the apostle?

IN CLOSING

• What is the image of God you have as a result of reading Ephesians 2:1-10? How would you summarize what it means to be dead in sin, a condition open to all persons?

• Close with prayer for all those who live in the darkness of sin they feel unable to escape; pray for their willingness to let God into that abyss. Pray for your own discipline of obedience to Christ to accept the immeasurable riches of his grace.

VI No Longer Strangers and Aliens

Christ, Our Peace
Read Ephesians 2:11-22

Ephesians turns from the generalized picture of salvation to the heart of Paul's message. Christ came to unite all humans in God's people. The ancient division between Jew and non-Jew had been abolished.

Once again the author speaks to his Gentile audience from the Jewish point of view. According to the writer, before converting to Christianity, Gentiles had no chance of salvation (compare Romans 1:18-32). Of course, Jews who lived alongside Gentiles in the cities of Asia Minor knew that individual Gentiles were capable of acts of moral virtue. Paul says as much in Romans 2:10-16. God may even reward people whose lives correspond to the righteousness revealed in the Torah.

Such exceptions do not speak to the theological point posed by a covenant theology, however. From that point of view, God has called a people into the covenant. Circumcision and the Torah are signs of a community's life in relationship with God. Blessings, peace or well-being (*shalom*), are the response of a merciful, loving, and faithful God (see Exodus 34:6-7). As Paul's missionary work drew Gentiles to God through Christ, the apostle became convinced that the terms of God's covenant promise were not as he had once thought, exclusive to Israel. Instead, Paul reached back behind the Sinai covenant to the covenant between God and Abraham. God's plan was not to divide the world between Jew and Gentile, but to unite both as heirs to those promises in Christ (see Romans 3:21–5:21).

However, this union faced a number of barriers, including the prevalent practice of idol worship among the Gentiles and the exterior threat of Roman persecution if this Christianity attempted to usurp the role and value of the Roman gods.

Speaking to the wealthy cities of Roman Asia Minor, this gospel had special meaning. The established temples to gods and goddesses, especially the famous Artemis shrine at Ephesus (see Acts 19:23-41), were getting some competition. Augustus began a tradition of Roman building in these cities that would glorify imperial rule. Among those structures attributed to his reign, we find a rebuilt market area with ceremonial gates, a town hall, and a double temple dedicated to Julius Caesar and Rome. A new street linked the renovated 25,000-seat theater to the harbor. Three new aqueducts brought water in for the growing population and supplied newly constructed Roman baths, which also served as gathering places. So far, six have been uncovered in Ephesus.

Augustus claimed that his rule brought peace to the diverse peoples of the Empire. That message was built into the very architecture of the ancient city. Who could fail to be impressed? At the same time, the population in port cities like Corinth and Ephesus was as diverse as in any modern city. The new civic temples and public spaces played a critical role in uniting the mix. Acts 19:23-41 attributes riots over Paul's preaching to economic losses suffered by declining tourist trade at the Artemis shrine. Luke may be seeking to downplay the danger Christians faced if the new faith was seen as a threat to Roman order.

Yet we cannot escape the significance of what Ephesians is saying. The true civic concord is not in Augustus. It is not in the Jerusalem Temple either. The "dividing wall" between Jew and non-Jew (Ephesians 2:14) is both a metaphor for the Law and an allusion to an architectural structure. Gentiles were kept from the inner courts of the Jerusalem Temple by a wall. Trespassers were threatened with death. Paul was arrested in Jerusalem on the suspicion that he had taken one of his Gentile converts into the forbidden area (Acts 21:27-36). In fact, the individual in question was from Ephesus. So you can see that this passage in Ephesians has very dramatic overtones.

This passage also suggests that the author of Ephesians is looking forward to the next generation. He speaks of the church as "built upon the foundation of the apostles and prophets" (Ephesians 2:20). And this new community has its own building to celebrate. But the building is not made of stones and mortar like the new Roman architecture. This building is the people of God who are in Christ, "joined together and grow[ing] into a holy temple in the Lord" (2:21). It is a new unity of people in God's Spirit, not in buildings, politics, and economics. That is as difficult a vision to sell today as it was in the first century. In fact, perhaps it was even more difficult in the first century. Not a single public monument stood for this new kind of peace. Roman imperial rule was visible everywhere.

CHRIST, OUR PEACE

• What buildings in your community define civic identity? (In my area, a huge, expensive highway project, "The Big Dig"—a sinkhole for money—and a new baseball stadium, "Fenway Park"—a problem of neighborhood and perhaps also of name—define civic identity.)
• What happens when a corporate sponsor wants to put its name on a revered arena or field?
• Where do churches, mosques, or synagogues fit into our civic space? (In my New England town, the presence and influence of specific denominations or other religious groups are clustered in observable patterns.) What religious story is told in your town buildings?
• Read Ephesians 2:11-22 and Acts 19:23-41. How has Ephesians combined the image of the church as "body of Christ" with building metaphors to describe the peace that comes when a divided humanity is brought together in Christ? What does it mean to you no longer to be a stranger or alien but a member of God's household?
• How do we use our church buildings to promote unity and peace in our community?

Prisoner for the Gospel
Read Ephesians 3:1-13

The author of Ephesians emphasizes the drama of this new message by having Paul, the prisoner, connect his mission to the Gentiles with divine revelation. Apparently the readers are familiar with earlier letters of the apostle. "As I wrote above in a few words" (Ephesians 3:3b) probably does not refer to Ephesians 2:11-22, but to what Paul had written previously in Colossians or perhaps to a collection of Paul's letters. Notice that he attributes knowledge of the divine mystery—that Gentiles are to become part of the same people of God with Jews—to "the apostles and prophets" (3:5-6). The fierce debates between Paul and other Christian apostles on whether and under what conditions Gentiles could be included (see Galatians 1–2) have faded into the past. Ephesians admits that this "mystery" required a new revelation by God. By just reading their Scriptures, the Jewish people could never conclude that God would include non-Jews or that God would end the rule of the Torah commandments that separated the people of God from outsiders (Ephesians 2:15).

Even though the author of Ephesians is a Jewish Christian, the struggle over whether the Law should retain a place in Christian communities seems to be over; and so does immediate hostility from local synagogues (contrast 1 Thessalonians 2:14-16). Consequently, Ephesians implies that the Jewish descendants of Abraham were welcoming non-Jews (Ephesians 2:6). There is no polemical edge to the treatment of Israel in Ephesians (contrast Galatians 3:6–4:31). Nor does Ephesians wish to imply that its message of universal humanity in Christ might provoke civic discord. It only challenged the superstitious devotion to stars, demons, and magical powers and the general immorality of Gentiles. Nothing is said about the great temples and civic forms of religion, though everyone knew that Jews refused allegiance to them. Christians must do the same.

This tone creates something of a puzzle as the imprisoned apostle presents himself to the reader. Why is he in jail? Ephesians never offers an explanation. One might infer from 6:11-12 that demonic powers are responsible. Ephesians has taken the content of this depiction from Colossians 1:23-28 but omits the link between the suffering apostle and the cross of Christ (as in Colossians 1:24). Ephesians also reformulates the language of God's power at work so that it bypasses the characteristic Pauline motif of the power of God manifest in suffering (Ephesians 3:7; compare Colossians 1:29; also see 2 Corinthians 12:7b-10).

In Colossians the "working" (Greek, *energeia*) is "in me,"

that is, the apostle who is suffering for the gospel. In Ephesians, God's powerful activity is manifest in the grace by which Paul was called to be apostle to the Gentiles — a subtle shift, perhaps, but one that shows how the image of the apostle was beginning to change in the years after his death. He is to be remembered as a heroic figure, not as a degraded or controversial one. So as the section concludes, the readers are encouraged to remember Paul's sufferings as "your glory" (Ephesians 3:13).

This exhortation attaches to a concern that Paul's imprisonment might lead to discouragement among the Gentile churches. Why? Ephesians does not explain. Perhaps the author recognizes that a future without the apostles is perilous and discouraging; perhaps he fears his addressees would face persecution as well. But note that Paul seems to have taught his converts to expect "persecution" (1 Thessalonians 1:6-7; Greek, *thlipsis*, used in Ephesians 3:13 for Paul's imprisonment).

What is the "glory" that Ephesians expects Christians to experience, thanks to Paul's suffering? Since the author does not use the term *boast* (as Paul did in 2 Corinthians 11:30, for example), scholars do not think that he meant to make Paul a hero-figure. Ephesians may have the cosmic body of Christ in view as the "glory" that believers receive thanks to Paul's efforts (compare Paul's use of "death in us" and "life in you" in 2 Corinthians 4:12; similarly 2 Corinthians 1:6; 2 Timothy 2:10). But verse 13 contains one of those odd shifts in phrase that alerts readers that another writer is using Paul's voice.

Paul can speak of his sufferings as a sacrificial offering for the faith of his converts (as in Philippians 2:17), but he does not claim that these sufferings are to God's glory. Paul's boast, crown of victory, and glory will be the faith of Christians in the churches his mission established (Philippians 2:16; 1 Thessalonians 2:19-20, "you are our glory and joy"). After the apostle's death, this personal appeal to his converts is no longer possible. Instead, Paul's faithful suffering for the gospel becomes the glory of all Christians, even those who do not belong to churches the apostle founded.

PRISONER FOR THE GOSPEL

- List images or characteristics that you associate with Paul. Do you have pictures of the apostle in your mind? If so, what do they look like?
- How many of your images evoke suffering or imprisonment? How many depict glory?
- We have a stained glass window that shows Paul with a big sword. To the kids it means that Paul was like a gladiator or like Luke Skywalker. They would give Paul the ever-popular light sword! What about your children and youth?
- Does the image of a Christian hero need to be updated for the 21st century? If so, how?
- Paul describes himself as "very least of all the saints" (3:8) yet entrusted with a key understanding of and role in God's plan of salvation. Does this image of humility square with your view of Paul?
- Ephesians evokes the greatness of the gospel with which Paul is entrusted. How does an extraordinary message, one destined to affect all human beings, produce humility in its servants?
- Do you agree that Paul was in awe of what God was accomplishing through his mission? Explain.
- In what way are you a servant of the gospel?

Prayer Report
Read Ephesians 3:14-21

Another prayer report asks God to complete the work of salvation in the hearts and minds of the readers (Ephesians 3:16-19) and concludes with a doxology (3:20-21). The kneeling posture is unusual. Ordinarily persons in Paul's day stood to pray. Supplicants knelt before a powerful person when making a request (see Mark 1:40; 10:17). Luke has persons kneeling to pray when they are about to die (Luke 22:41, Jesus; Acts 7:60, Stephen; Acts 20:36 and 21:5, Paul). If the letter's recipients know this convention, then Ephesians highlights the fact that this may be Paul's final prayer for his churches in Asia Minor. The address to God links the designation "Father" (Greek, pat_r) with the word *patria*, which means "clan, race, descendants of a common ancestor." Instead of the NRSV translation "family," some commentators propose translating *patria* as "social grouping."

Why refer to "Father" as a way of saying that God is the origin of every race or social group? Many ancient Roman clans traced their ancestry back to a divine or semi-divine ancestor. Remember that temple to Julius Caesar and Rome that Augustus had built in Ephesus? That was a way of saying that Augustus' predecessor was a semi-divine founder of the imperial family. Jewish families went back to the twelve patriarchs. So Ephesians may wish to stress the unity of all humanity in God's plan. Or the writer may wish to counter some pagan practices that used divine names in magic or astrology.

The prayer as a whole builds toward a climax in Ephesians 3:19. Only by receiving the "fullness of God," a reference to God's Spirit (5:18; or possibly to God's love, 3:17), can the readers understand the cosmic dimensions of the love that God has shown in Christ (compare Romans 8:31-38).

The final doxology has an unusual feature. Ephesians introduces the church as the place in which glory is offered to God. This modification fits the heavenly significance of the church already described in Ephesians 1:22-23. The glory that the church possesses is reflected glory.

It is God's glory in Christ, not some human achievement. But as God's glory it outshines anything that the Roman emperor had to offer. The doxology serves as a conclusion to the theological section of the letter (compare Romans 11:26). Now that readers have been challenged to apprehend God's universal plan of salvation, Ephesians turns to instruction in Christian living.

PRAYER REPORT

• Clan ancestry, preferably descent from a heroic or semi-divine figure, played an important role in ancient society. At the funeral of a prominent Roman aristocrat, masks of noble ancestors were carried in procession. How do ancestors function in your family? Do you have portraits, pictures, letters, diaries, or other items handed down from famous (or notorious) ancestors?

• How does your experience of ancestry influence your response to the proclamation that every clan takes its name from God (Ephesians 3:15)? Does it matter whether you imagine God as the ancestral patriarch or the ancestral matriarch? Explain.

• Suggesting a change in posture for prayer can divide any congregation. How many different postures do you use in church? in private prayer?

• How many postures for prayer can you imagine for your own and other religions? Did you include any that involve movements?

• The most common posture for prayer in ancient Christian art is the *orans*, a standing figure with arms raised up and palms facing outward. How does that figure differ from kneeling as an adequate prayer posture? Remember Paul is a chained prisoner in Ephesians. How do you imagine him uttering this prayer?

IN CLOSING

• Look carefully at this prayer in Ephesians 3:14-19. Pray together for all the saints to have the power to comprehend the breadth, length, height, and depth of the love of Christ and to act on it faithfully.

• Close by saying together Ephesians 3:19-20 as a benediction.

Bust of Nero
© 1986 Biblical Archaeology Society

VII THE OLD LIFE AND THE NEW

Walk Worthily
Read Ephesians 4:1-6

Paul's letters always follow the theological section with advice on how to live as a Christian. Ephesians 4:1 reminds the audience that it is the imprisoned apostle who stands behind these words. Even though salvation comes through God's gracious power, not through human reform efforts (Ephesians 2:1-10), Christians are obliged to exhibit God's holiness in their lives (2:10; 1:4). This opening salvo combines a brief list of virtues (4:2-3) with a well-known formulation that appeals to the unity of God and faith (4:4-6). Items in the list—humility, gentleness, patience, bearing with one another in love—are drawn from Colossians 3:12-15. This list is oriented toward demonstrating that the virtues of Christian community support its claim that Christ is the source of universal peace (Ephesians 2:17).

This emphasis explains why the virtues are directed toward life in the community rather than toward outsiders. Contrast Romans 12:9-21, which moves from relationships between Christians to living peacefully with outsiders who may be hostile to believers. The unity formula in Ephesians 4:4-6 grounds the appeal for concord in both the nature of the church as the body of Christ and the nature of God—Spirit, Lord, God and Father of all. Earlier, God as "Father" was used to ground a theological claim about the unity of all humanity (3:14-15).

WALK WORTHILY

• The opening words in Ephesians 4:1-6, "I beg," are best understood as words of encouragement, not as words of pleading or scolding. Does the tone in which someone offers advice have any influence on your willingness to follow the advice? Explain.

• Do you associate the ethical sections of Paul's letters with scolding or with encouragement? Why? Are you more likely to listen to someone who is suffering for the faith like Paul than to someone who seems to have everything?

• How many expressions of unity can you find in Ephesians 4:1-6? How is unity related to the nature and activity of God?

• Remember the architecture of the ancient city. It was filled with statues, shrines, and temples to gods and heroes. How does this section of Ephesians reinforce belief in the one God? What competes with monotheism in our cities?

Gifts of Christ
Read Ephesians 4:7-16

Ephesians 4:7-16 develops Paul's vision of the church as a body in which each person has a special part (compare 1 Corinthians 12:4-31). All must work together in harmony for the body to flourish. Maybe we do not think about how important that is until some part of the body is not working. Even a fairly minor injury can throw everything off. Paul used the word *gift* (Greek, *charisma*) to stress the work of the Spirit in unifying the local church because the Corinthians were competing over spiritual gifts (1 Corinthians 12:1, 11).

Ephesians substitutes the word *grace* (Greek, *charis*) and shifts the perspective to the church as a universal community with Christ at its head. This shift enables Ephesians to introduce the idea of the church as a body that has to grow up, to become mature, "to the measure of the full stature of Christ" (Ephesians 4:13). Through unity and mutual love the body grows into its head, Christ (4:15-16). To pick a human example, the head is the biggest thing about a new baby. The rest of the body has to catch up. When the proportions get shifted around and the child is running and talking, we suddenly notice that he or she is not a baby any longer.

Of course, Ephesians gives us a much more dramatic perspective. It even interrupts cataloging the gifts to toss in a bit of early Christian theology. Verse 8 quotes Psalm 68:18). Then Ephesians 4:9-10 interprets the psalm as a prediction of Christ's triumphant exaltation in heaven after his resurrection. This exaltation has already been described as filling the entire cosmos (4:10; 1:23; 3:19). This image makes the gifts bestowed on the body (4:11-16) even more dramatic. It is as if they are bestowed on the entire cosmos. "Apostles, prophets and evangelists" appear to be figures from the first generation of the Christian mission, while pastors and teachers are permanent fixtures in the church (4:11; 2:20; 3:5). From Colossians 2:2-4, Ephesians knows that false teaching remains a permanent danger to the growth and unity of the church. Unlike Colossians, Ephesians does not appear to have any particular crisis of false teaching in view. It remains the responsibility of all Christians to grow in their faith so that they cannot be taken in by every religious fad that comes along.

GIFTS OF CHRIST

• Recently I heard an organizational management guru solemnly announce that the best companies had community spirit. In a community people work because of what they can contribute, not because of what they get. How do you react when someone gets paid big bucks in corporate America for such recycled Christian wisdom?

• What happens when you are asked to contribute your gifts to the church community? Do you fall into attitudes about community picked up at work?

• Sociologists observe that Americans are paying for services we used to do ourselves. Have we taken that attitude into our church community? Are only paid staff responsible for a healthy church? (Ephesians would say no.)

• For a body to grow, all the parts have to be active. How is your activity level?

• What gifts do you bring to your community of faith? How often do you get to offer them? How well do you do so?

Two Ways of Life
Read Ephesians 4:17-32

Ephesians 4:17-32 adopts a common form of ethical exhortation contrasting a past way of life marked by ignorance and vice (4:18-19, 22) with the new life of virtue (4:20-21, 23-24). This introduction does not mean that the audience was returning to its old ways. Rather such teaching was part of the ongoing process of moral formation. It was necessary for those making progress in virtue. Only persons in whom virtue had reached such perfection that it could not be shaken would fail to need such encouragement. Notice the shift in language. Earlier the Jewish Christian author had addressed readers as "you Gentiles" (2:11), indicating their non-Jewish origins. Now, thinking of humanity as divided between those who know God and those who do not, Ephesians tells them to separate themselves from the immorality of the Gentiles (4:17; similarly 1 Peter 2:12). Much of the language in this section recalls earlier exhortations in Romans 1:21, 24 and Colossians 3:5-10.

Ephesians 4:25–5:2 contains brief statements of virtues to be adopted and vices to be avoided. Most of the items are familiar Pauline teaching (compare Colossians 3:8-9, 12–13; Romans 12:14-21). Most of these pithy sayings concern evils that originate with speech and its consequences of anger, bitterness, and the like (Ephesians 4:25-27, 29, 31-32). Appropriate speech, truthfulness, words of encouragement, reconciliation, and forgiveness build up the community.

Verse 25 uses Zechariah 8:16 (from Colossians 3:8-9) to commend speaking truth to the neighbor; but the concluding tag, "for we are members of one another," seems to limit the horizon to fellow Christians. This limit is probably a consequence of the author's focus on the moral life as building up the body of Christ. Ephesians 4:26 opens with Psalm 4:4 and then advises that to be angry without sin requires shedding anger before sundown. Do not brood or even "sleep on it"! Ephesians 4:31-32 puts this teaching against anger within the Christian framework of grace received.

Two items seem out of place in this discussion: theft (Ephesians 4:28) and grieving the Holy Spirit (4:30). First Corinthians 6:10 includes thieves in a list of those who will not inherit the Kingdom (similarly 1 Peter 4:15). Why might such an injunction come up? We have no reason to think that the addressees were ex-criminals. But remember Onesimus. Philemon 18 hints that he had stolen from his master. That may be the kind of pilfering Ephesians has in mind (also see Titus 2:10). Slaves and hired servants often faced such accusations. Unfortunately, we find a similar climate in many businesses today. Employees who would never regard themselves as thieves think nothing of walking off with valuable computer equipment, supplies, or abusing other company resources. (Such behavior is not limited to low-wage earners, either.)

Ephesians repeats one of Paul's persistent bits of advice. Every Christian should follow his example, working at a job to earn a living (1 Corinthians 9:6; 2 Thessalonians 3:6-13). True to the overarching theme of the section, the motivation for working is to have something to give to the needy. Think about that when stewardship appeal rolls around. That paycheck is not just for us or for our families. We are to use it to build up the body of Christ by providing for those in need.

Ephesians 4:30 is more of a puzzle. The expression echoes Isaiah 63:10: "They rebelled and grieved his Holy Spirit." In this instance, however, the Holy Spirit is not an indirect reference to God but refers to the Spirit received by believers in their "one baptism" (Ephesians 4:5). When members of the Jewish sect the Essenes referred to "defiling" the Holy Spirit received from God, they had in mind departing from the ritual, legal, and moral precepts of the Law. Ephesians may have something like this in mind.

TWO WAYS OF LIFE

• This passage formulates a sharp contrast between the ignorance, greed, and general moral decay of the "Gentiles" (non-believers) on the one hand and the holiness, justice, and spirit of Christians on the other. List the characteristics of each type of life. Which is more attractive? Which pieces of advice do you find hardest to follow?

• This passage formulates a sharp contrast between the ignorance, greed, and general moral decay of the "Gentiles" (non-believers) on the one hand and the holiness, justice, and spirit of Christians on the other. List the characteristics of each type of life. Which is more attractive? Which pieces of advice do you find hardest to follow?

• A meeting with parents after small group sessions with seventh and eighth graders focused on the gap between saying that people should tolerate differences and be accepting of others and the sometimes poor way these youngsters treated one another. "They don't even notice how mean they are," one mother remarked. Maybe none of us do. How can we use this teaching on speech to become more aware of how we actually treat others?

• Paul's teaching on work reminds us that nothing is outside the scope of Christian discipleship. What do you think your paycheck is for? Is giving to others a necessary budget item, or is it a luxury? Why?

• I know some people who will not join a church because they know they will be asked to contribute money. How would you respond to someone who said that?

Imitate God
Read Ephesians 5:1-2

This exhortation to imitate God stands between the catalog of virtues that distinguish Christian life from the moral ignorance of the "Gentiles" (Ephesians 4:17-32) and another reminder that as children of light, Christians must reject all forms of vice (5:3-18). You will find these exhortations attached to one section or the other in different editions of the New Testament. These two verses urge believers to treat others with kindness because of the goodness God has shown us, from 4:32, and reformulate it as the commandment to love others as Christ has loved us in giving up his life (5:2). It was a commonplace in ancient moral exhortation that the young should find models of virtue to imitate. Parents and teacher-philosophers were expected to fit that bill.

Paul told readers to learn from his example how they should imitate Christ (see 1 Corinthians 4:16; 11:1; 1 Thessalonians 1:6; 2 Thessalonians 3:7, 9). Ephesians has generalized the topic by omitting the appeal to apostolic example. Christians are to look to the sacrifice of Jesus as a model for love (Ephesians 2:4; 3:19; compare John 13:34-35; 15:9-13). The injunction to imitate God can be found nowhere else in the New Testament.

IMITATE GOD

- What does it mean to you to imitate God? If we cannot be perfect as God is, what point is there in suggesting that we imitate God?
- Does Jesus' sacrifice of himself motivate you to live in love? Explain.

Live as Children of Light
Read Ephesians 5:3-14

The shift from Christ's "fragrant offering" (Ephesians 5:2) to "fornication" (5:3) is somewhat jarring. The mental association may have been the ritual purity and sweet smell of rituals (incense and flowers cover up the nasty smells of animal sacrifices) as the opposite of impurity, which is present in the vice list (5:3-5; compare Colossians 3:5-8). This list repeats items from the previous section: Immorality is the consequence of idol worship (Ephesians 5:5; 4:18), greed (5:3, 5; 4:19), and unguarded and immoral speech (5:4; 4:29).

Ephesians 5:6-14 organizes the exhortation to a moral life around another familiar topic: light against darkness or children of light against children of disobedience. Again, the warning against deceivers (5:6) appears to be a generalization rather than a reference to some specific threat facing the addressees. The warning against having anything to do with immoral persons (5:7, 11-12) repeats advice that Paul gave the Corinthians (see 1 Corinthians 5:9-13). Looking back to that earlier example, we see that he did not mean for Christians to isolate themselves from non-Christian society. Because the Pauline letters share the Jewish assumption that worshiping idols rather than God is associated with other vices (see Romans 1:18-32), they assume that non-believers are trapped in immorality. Paul is concerned with Christians who are indifferent to the moral evils in their life.

Ephesians does not note this distinction. Paul only did so in 1 Corinthians 5:9 because a previous letter had been misunderstood. However, Ephesians' ethical section as a whole looks to the building up of the church. Ephesians 5:3 enjoins that vices such as sexual immorality and greed should not even be spoken of among Christians. Vulgar speech should be replaced by prayer and hymns of thanksgiving (5:4, 19). So when the letter speaks of avoiding persons who do such things and exposing immorality to the light (5:13), we may conclude that this image refers to correcting fellow Christians.

Should that restriction exist today? Some people use the principle of separation of church and state to drive a wedge between faith-based ethical convictions and public discourse. Others point out that even though Christians have a particular energy and concern behind their quest for justice, for peace, for charity towards the poor and the like, the vices that Christians name still harm everyone. So we can reasonably expect people of faith to point the spotlight on evil wherever they encounter it.

Some scholars have recently suggested that the equation of sexual immorality and pagan idolatry should be taken as reference to the threat of pagan religious cults. Paul had to warn Christians against thinking that they could attend banquets at pagan temples (see 1 Corinthians 10:1-22). In Ephesians 5:3-14, obscene talk and secret gestures performed in darkness, rites that no one is permitted to mention, could refer to a different form of religion. Therefore these scholars think that Ephesians is warning Christians against joining groups that conduct such secret rites. Everything Christians do belongs in the full light of day (5:9-14a).

The light image concludes with a piece of poetry (5:14b). The introduction, "therefore it says," shows that what follows is a quotation; but its source is not clear. Presumably the death from which the sleeper is to awaken is death in sin. The image may be baptismal (Romans 6:4) or eschatological (1 Thessalonians 5:5-8; Romans 13:11-14—While others sleep, Christians are awake anticipating the day of the Lord.).

LIVE AS CHILDREN OF LIGHT

• Ephesians presumes that sinners seek the cover of darkness. Do you agree? Is it somehow more offensive when someone publicly flaunts some immorality or inappropriate behavior rather than keeping it a secret? Explain.

• When Ephesians recommends that Christians expose works of darkness to the light, is public exposure what is meant? Have you ever stumbled on hidden immorality at work, in school, by a public figure, by a friend's spouse? What did you do?

• Assuming that Ephesians does not refer to some secret religious cult, why does the author advise Christians not to talk about greed, sexual immorality, obscenity, and other so-called "works of darkness"? How can we educate and counsel if some subjects are taboo?

Wisdom Is Giving Thanks
Read Ephesians 5:15-20

A new warning plays off the contrast between the foolish and the wise (Ephesians 6:15; compare Colossians 4:5). The exhortation to recognize the critical moment (Ephesians 5:16; Greek, *kairos*) suggests an eschatological reading of verse 14. Christians live in the "evil days" at the end of the age, so they must take special care to discern the will of God (5:17). "Drunkenness" is a commonplace image among ancient moralists for persons trapped by vice (5:18). Ephesians employs "filled with the Spirit" as its antithesis to vice and to make a transition back to the topic of Christian speech—specifically the joyful music and thanksgiving of Christian worship (5:19-20; compare Colossians 3:16-17).

We tend to discuss music and ethics only when the two are at odds, as in the lyrics of some forms of rap. We may also be inspired by the music sung in church and have our favorite hymn tunes. But we usually think that the serious business of shaping good Christian lives is done in sermons, in words rather than in music. Yet we realize how profound a spiritual effect music can have on us. Most of us use music to help babies and little kids (and ourselves) get through all sorts of emotional crises, from going to sleep to anger and boredom. Ephesians suggests that we expand our range. Christian wisdom is in singing hearts (Ephesians 5:19).

WISDOM IS GIVING THANKS

• Every now and then one hears about playing Mozart to children to make them better at math. What about music can help us be better persons?

• What kind of music might help you in your moral development? How could it help?

• We often use music to soothe young children and to affect their behavior. How does music function in your house? (My 3½-year-old nephew was very proud of the xylophone concert he put on to help the plumber fix the kitchen sink. His music was preferable to his advice, also offered!)

• Should, or could, music be substituted for pestering advice?

IN CLOSING

• In what ways is "being filled with the Spirit" exhibited in your church, particularly in your worship services?

• Close with prayer for the presence of the wise Spirit to guide and lead you and others away from evil and toward the light.

• Sing or say together a favorite hymn, perhaps one that focuses on the activity of the Holy Spirit.

VIII THE HOUSEHOLD OF GOD

Household Order
Read Ephesians 5:21–6:9

One might expect the language of praise to conclude the exhortation, since it ends in praise to God, the Father, through Christ (Ephesians 5:20). However, Ephesians inserts a formally distinct unit of ethical instruction, rules, or advice on the well-ordered household (see Colossians 3:18–4:1 and related material in 1 Peter 2:18–3:7; Titus 2:1-10). This familiar topic in philosophical preaching presumed that household order was a training ground for order in society at large. Hence order requires the proper respect and subordination of inferiors (wives, slaves, children) to those over them (husbands, masters, fathers). That premise is behind the recommendation that wives "be subject" (Greek, *hypotassesthai*) to their husband (Ephesians 5:22; Colossians 3:18). This verb has an unpleasant ring for modern Christians who are used to thinking of marriage as a partnership based on equality and mutual respect. Ephesians 5:21 connects the household code with the earlier exhortation by formulating a general principle of conduct. Christians are to be "subject" to one another.

No one in ancient society would have blinked an eye at the idea that obedience to one's superior is the best way to order things. Since a modern democratic society requires different skills, such as mutual respect, ability to appreciate different viewpoints, and compromise, Christians today should not be shy about applying these democratic virtues to family relationships. The best families are not those in which everyone is forced to obey the rigid orders of the father—especially if that authority is backed up with violence. But we also know that endless disputes, conflict, and the insistence of all family members on going their own way does not work either. Parents have to agree on basic rules for their children. Husbands and wives have to decide who is in charge of various areas of family life. And those arrangements may shift with particular interests, expertise, or work schedules so that they are not as obviously linked to gender as in the past.

The section of the household code that refers to slaves and masters (6:5-8) has less obvious application to our lives. Remember Paul wrote to Philemon asking him for leniency toward his slave Onesimus, who had converted to Christianity. Christian household codes ask Christian slaves to prove that they are not like the ordinary slaves—liable to defraud the master behind his back, lazy, and flatterers to boot (compare Colossians 3:22-23; 1 Peter 2:18; Titus 2:9-10).

Today some people think of this advice as fostering the oppression of those who were enslaved. In antiquity, slaves were of all races. They had a wide range of occupations. Some had major educational and business experience. When freed by their masters, former slaves still had ties to their prior owner. Many became wealthy and even participated in imperial administration. Most of the slaves envisaged here are household slaves, not those condemned to hard labor.

By presuming that Christian slaves could have virtues

that lifted them above the ordinary prejudices of their society, these codes do say something positive. Slaves are moral persons even if their owners can treat them as things. Masters are warned that they will be accountable to God for the way in which they treat their slaves. So we could translate this advice into more modern terms. We may not be slaves, but many of us have jobs that involve serving a wide variety of (sometimes difficult and officious) people. This advice asks us to be friendly, sincere, and helpful. Others are bosses. We too have to treat those under us as persons who have standing with God.

The most unusual section of the household order in Ephesians comes when the author turns to the relationship between husbands and wives (Ephesians 5:22-33). The shorter rules of Colossians 3:18-19 have been expanded by a metaphorical translation from husbands and wives to Christ and the church (Ephesians 5:23-27) and through that to the bodily unity of husbands and wives based on Genesis 2:24 (Ephesians 5:28-31). The conclusion treats the Christ and church image as theological speculation on God's plan ("a mystery"; 5:32).

Asked to draw the final moral, Ephesians requires that husbands love their wives as themselves and that wives respect their husbands (5:33). Howls of protest greet this passage whenever it comes up in the Sunday readings. The objections reflect a misuse of the text to enforce a social view of wives as dependent upon the authority of their husbands. Or worse, its citation by clergy, parents, or others has encouraged women to put up with abusive treatment in marriage.

Consider making the metaphorical substitutions that Ephesians does. Would Christ as head of the church be angry, jealous, physically abusive, or suppress the human

growth and well-being of its members? Absurd, of course!
Ephesians reminds readers that Christ sacrificed his own
life for the church (5:25). Then what does it mean to take
Genesis 2:24 (a man and woman become one flesh) as
a description of the relationship between a husband and
his wife? When the one flesh they become is his (or hers),
we have a distortion of the unity and bond between them.
The claim that this text contributes to oppression of
women or family violence is not based on the religious
message found in the Scripture. In fact, the metaphors
that Ephesians uses might serve as a litmus test for how
we treat our wife or husband.

What led Ephesians to apply the metaphors of Christ as
head of the church and "one flesh" to the household code
for husbands and wives? Commentators remain unsure.
However, the Genesis 2:24 text appears in debates over
divorce on the side of those who argue against divorce for
any reason the parties may choose. Both the pious Jews
(see Malachi 2:16) and the Gospels (see Matthew 19:5)
refer to Genesis 2:24 in this context. Paul used Genesis
2:24 in 1 Corinthians 6:16 to argue that Christians should
not consider sex with prostitutes as morally indifferent.
Such sexual activity violates the unity that they have as
Christians with Christ as members of his body
(1 Corinthians 6:15). Thus Paul may have taken what had
been part of the legal debate about marriage and used it to
address other questions of sexual morality.

The Pauline teacher who wrote Ephesians had already
picked up the image of church as body of Christ in his
reflection on the cosmic scope of salvation (see Ephesians
1:22-23). Given the use of Genesis 2:24 and "body of
Christ" in 1 Corinthians 6:15, the household code instructions on marriage may have seemed a natural place to

develop the imagery further, just as Ephesians 4:15-16 applied the metaphor to the growth of the church in love.

Ancient readers could also hear echoes of the legal tradition of the marriage contract. Marriage contracts often spelled out the husband's responsibilities to provide his wife with appropriate food, home, and clothing. The comment on the husband "nourishing" his own flesh in 5:29 might evoke that terminology. But transposed into the Christian context, "nourish" means much more than to fulfill one's contractual obligation. Christ's care for the church results in a body that is spotless in holiness and beauty (6:26-27), and that union is sacramental in nature.

When the author of Ephesians refers to the metaphor of Christ and the church as a "mystery" in 5:32, he has taken over a term that Paul used for God's plan of salvation as revealed in Christ (Romans 11:25; 1 Corinthians 2:7; 15:51; Colossians 1:24-26). Ephesians 3:3-4 depicted the apostle as the one who has made that mystery of salvation known among the Gentiles (also Ephesians 1:9; 3:9; compare 1 Corinthians 4:1). The Greek word *mySt_rion* was translated *sacramentum* in some versions of the Latin text. That translation provided impetus for including marriage as a sacrament of the church, not merely a legal contract between two persons.

Ephesians 6:2-3 also expands the advice to children with a reference to the Ten Commandments (Exodus 20:12; contrast Colossians 3:20). Jewish exegesis from the time of Jesus shows that the command to honor one's parents was applied to adults. No one could plead exemption from providing for them in their old age. However, Ephesians 6:4 admonishes parents to educate their children, so the author does not appear to have adult children in view. In contrast to earlier Pauline letters in which only one parent might be a Christian (see 1 Corinthians 7:12-16), Ephesians presumes that both parents are believers. They no longer instruct their children in the old moral values of society that required even adult children to obey parents (as in Colossians 3:20-21). Instead, Christian parents are to instruct children in the Christian way of life (Ephesians 6:4).

HOUSEHOLD ORDER

• Review the unit on the household order in Colossians 3:18–4:1 and Ephesians 5:21–6:9. What differences do the expansions in Ephesians make to your understanding of this material?

• Does the lengthened instruction to husbands relieve or increase the charge of some feminists that the household codes foster a patriarchy of love, not development of women into full personhood? Explain.

• Both the comparison of marriage to Christ's love for the church (body of Christ) and the later translation of *myst_rion* as *sacramentum* helped develop the idea that a marriage between two Christians is something more than a legal contract. How is the Christian marriage covenant or sacrament different from a civil marriage?

• What should Christians do to prepare for such an agreement? What are the most important stipulations in your own covenantal relationship?

• Ephesians has repeatedly described the body of Christ as growing into its fullness. If we apply that insight to this reflection on marriage, how does marriage contribute to the growth of the husband and wife, the parents and children?

• How do we know when a marriage has died? Should we have an appropriate ritual to acknowledge an end to the covenant as we do to begin one? If so, what might it be?

Possessing the Power of God
Read Ephesians 6:10-20

Paul often concludes his letters with a reminder about the end time. Ephesians follows that tradition by describing the faithful Christian as a soldier armed for battle against spiritual powers of evil (6:10-17). This image makes a fitting conclusion to a letter that began with the triumph of Christ over all the powers in the cosmos (1:9-23). The description of spiritual armor combines a number of Old Testament images. Each piece of armor represents a particular virtue.

• Ephesians 6:14 refers to the **belt of truth** (compare Isaiah 11:5 on righteousness and faithfulness as the belt) and **the breastplate of righteousness** (Isaiah 59:17; Wisdom of Solomon 5:18, Apocrypha).

• Ephesians 6:15 refers to the **shoes**, or the military sandals, **as a means to arrive at the gospel of peace** (Isaiah 52:7, the feet of the messenger who announces peace).

• Ephesians 6:16 refers to the **shield of faith** (Wisdom of Solomon 5:19, holiness as an invincible shield).

• Ephesians 6:17 refers to the **helmet of salvation** (Isaiah 59:17; Wisdom of Solomon 5:18, impartial justice as a helmet) and to the **sword of the Spirit** or Word of God (Isaiah 49:2, my mouth like a sharp sword).

Once again, Ephesians has expanded an earlier Pauline letter. First Thessalonians 5:8 asks Christians to put on the breastplate of faith and love and the helmet that is the hope of salvation. The general image of taking up God's power as armor against evil appears in other first-century Jewish writers. Ephesians is striking only in the detail with which the picture has been painted. It is as though the author were gazing at an armed Roman foot soldier, perhaps from the troops stationed in the city, and checking off each piece of armor. Ephesians also looks to the military methods of besieging a city. The soldier must be ready to meet flaming arrows flung down from above (Ephesians 6:16).

Certainly this is a rousing and dramatic ending, but one

that is troubling to many modern Christians. Perhaps first-century Christians really worried that they were under attack by spiritual beings or demonic forces, but are we required to believe that in the twenty-first century? Even in the first century, people often spoke of demons along-side negative internal passions that seemed to take over people's lives.

Novels, movies, and the even more incredible soap operas of everyday life should be enough to convince us that there are numerous forces that attack the life of faith. I noted a recent news story about an involuntary manslaughter charge against a mother and her boyfriend in the deaths of her five-and three-year-old children. The mother had passed out from cocaine use while the boyfriend played Nintendo. When the children's bedroom caught fire, he did nothing. By the time the mother roused and made a frantic 911 call, it was too late. In another story, a father was in such despair when his son died of leukemia that he committed suicide, leaving behind three other children. We are certainly not short of evil forces against which we need to take up God's power.

The last section of this conclusion brings readers back down to earth. Constant prayer is a staple of Christian life (Ephesians 6:18; also see 1:15-23; 3:14-21; Philippians 1:3-5; 4:6; 1 Thessalonians 5:17; Romans 1:8-10; Colossians 1:3-5; 4:12). Even more striking is the reminder that the apostle whose insight into God's plan of salvation has formed the faith of the letter's audience now lies in a Roman jail (Ephesians 6:19-20; compare Colossians 4:2-4, 18). Remember "chains" indicates a prisoner suffering the lowest, most degrading treatment. A dirty, ill-nourished figure asks readers to pray that he will still have the courage to speak boldly as an "ambassador" for the gospel.

We know from Philemon that when Paul was held under less severe forms of captivity, he did make prison an opportunity to bring others to the gospel. Luke imagines him doing the same at the conclusion to Acts (28:23-31). But Ephesians indicates a much worse scenario, with no sociable interaction with visitors. Nor could a chained prisoner baptize a fellow inmate. Paul still hopes to employ the high rhetoric of ambassador, but his physical situation makes that plea a near absurdity.

If, as many scholars think, Ephesians was actually written after the apostle's execution, the author may have put together this final image to instruct readers. No evidence survives that tells us how Paul came to be executed under Nero. But Ephesians paints a picture that would be familiar to first-century readers. Even the earlier description of spiritual armor set the scene. God's ambassador suffers in chains but will not be broken. That is God's power made visible.

POSSESSING THE POWER OF GOD

- A local news show went to the U.S. Army testing lab for a preview of what the infantry soldier of the future might be wearing—a suit that can change coloring, a high-tech helmet, fancy electronic communication gear and weaponry. The biggest hazards are the smallest: germs and chemical agents. How would we line up the armor of salvation with this picture of a soldier?
- Some things do not change. Armor is designed to protect against mortal wounds and to aid the soldier in killing others. Does the association with killing make "armed for battle" a problematic metaphor for Christian life? Explain.
- Should Christian parents discourage their children from playing war games, whether it is running around the yard with toy weapons or playing violent video games? Why? What about adults who like to reenact famous Revolutionary or Civil War battles?

• By ending with the image of Paul as a degraded ambassador in prison, Ephesians at least reminds us that battles have a cost. Spiritual, not physical, struggle is the way toward peace.

• If the military garb does not provide an acceptable image to you, how would you describe the tools and accoutrements that a good worker for God needs to do his or her work in the face of opposition? Draw or describe your model disciple.

• Germ and chemical agents present new problems for the military. Once the effects of these weapons are visible, it is too late to defend against them. Perhaps Ephesians could use such tactics as a metaphor for the Christian struggle against spiritual dangers. What are some of the invisible dangers, "wiles of the devil" (6:11), that Christians face?

• How do the virtues of this Christian armor keep these dangers from destroying faith?

• How are these virtues in Ephesians 6:10-20 related to one another?

• How are they supported by prayer?

Concluding Greetings
Read Ephesians 6:21-24

Ancient letters often end with a note that the bearer or someone else will be able to tell recipients more about the sender's situation. One might think that Tychicus supplied that vital missing information about Paul's last days (Ephesians 6:21-22). However, these words are almost an exact copy of Colossians 4:7-8; and, unlike Colossians, Ephesians contains no other names or personal greetings at the end. Instead, the final blessing is put in general terms. Any group of Christians who hear this letter read may see themselves as those "who have an undying love for our Lord Jesus Christ" (Ephesians 6:24).

Therefore, the ending of Ephesians supports the hypothesis that a follower or missionary associate of Paul composed the letter. Its author knew Colossians and other

Pauline letters very well. Perhaps the author sees Ephesians as a general summary of Paul's insight into the mystery of salvation for later Christians or for those churches in Asia Minor that did not have their own letters from Paul. Certainly, as we read the last verses, we can find ourselves among the people mentioned.

CONCLUDING GREETINGS

• How have you seen yourself as part of the Ephesians community? How do the concerns and advice expressed by the author touch your life?

• How would you describe the mystery of salvation?

• Do you see yourself as one who has "an undying love for our Lord Jesus Christ"? Explain.

IN CLOSING

• As you look at your own church experience, either in your local community or over the course of your life, how would you say that the "household" has been ordered? Was it orderly? mutually respectful? hierarchical or autocratic? Was it a place of health and growth or one of dysfunction and limitation?

• If your household portrait is not an inspiring one, what forces or circumstances made it that way, do you think? If it is a joyful and inspiring one, what forces or circumstances made it that way?

• Close in prayer for the health of all households, Christian or otherwise. Use Ephesians 6:23-24 as a benediction.